The BARK of DOG

Copyright © 2013 by Arf.

ALL RIGHTS RESERVED. No part of this work covered by the copyright hereon may be reproduced or used in any form or by any means—graphic, electronic, or mechanical, including photocopying, recording, taping, Web distribution, information storage and retrieval systems, or in any other manner—without the written permission of The BARK of DOG Foundation.

Published and distributed worldwide by **The BARK of DOG Foundation**, dedicated to helping homeless people and homeless dogs, to promoting peace, to teaching how to reason so people can think clearly from the heart, all through the way of DOG.

The BARK of DOG Foundation
P.O. Box 635
Socorro, NM 87801
USA
   www.TheBARKofDOG.org

Revised translation February, 2017.

ISBN
   Paperback   978-1-938421-15-0
   Hardback   978-1-938421-16-7
   e-book   978-1-938421-17-4

Introduction	1
In the Beginning	5
The Birth of NAV, the Only Puppy of DOG	11
The Ascension into Heaven of NAV, DOG's Only Puppy	15
The Preaching of St. Paw to the Gangesians	25
The Death of Juney	29
The Discovery of Boris, the Second DOGGY LAMA	37
The Pilgrimage of Tiny	43
She Who Loves the Lowest	49
The Great Schism	55
The Gift of Writing	69
Master Ts'en	75
Exodus	87
The Bringer of Drink	97
The Capture of Schadenfreude	103
In the Village of Sadhu-Shwa	109
Morton & Fletch Are Chosen	117
The Journey of Morton & Fletch	123
Morton & Fletch in the City of CAT	129
The Prophecy of Chica	139
Recent Writings	
At the Animal Shelter	149
A Report of a Parchment Inscription	155

Introduction

In 2001 an old man came to my home in the Middle Valley of the Rio Grande in New Mexico. He was short, slight, and burned from working in the sun. He wore a suit that was clearly new, though very cheap. His shoes were polished, though very worn. With black hair, parted at the side, he came bowed from what must have been much work in fields or with animals.

I do not know how he knew of me, of my dedication to DOG. But he knew. He spoke only a little English, and I spoke Portuguese, which was close enough to Spanish that we were able to communicate.

He came, he said, from a small village in the state of Chihuahua in Mexico, which for the safety of him and his fellow villagers I will not name. There, he told me, they have followed in the way of DOG for many generations, so many they cannot count nor remember who was the first. They have preserved the stories and the wisdom and the ways of DOG, he said, and of DOG's only Puppy, NAV. They know these, he said, by telling them at night as they share their food, the frijoles and maíz and chile, with sometimes a little meat from a rabbit; at the great holy days they slaughter a goat. They fear now because there are many narcotraficantes who demand that they help with the carrying of drugs and that they give their land to growing drugs. They resist but only in peace, they will not harm a human nor a dog. But the narcotraficantes are not moved, and those in the village fear now that their village will be no more.

They have protected for many generations, no one knows how long, what they are sure are writings of the way of DOG. They are written in a strange script on tabletas de oro, and he showed me one, a small tablet of gold, about 12 inches by 7 inches by 1 inch . It was beautiful, polished gold, shining with a kind of inner light. The others, he said, they have buried, they are afraid of the men with the guns who are greedy. This and this only he was able to bring to show me. It was gold, no doubt, it was solid gold. On it were a series of paw prints, tiny paw prints, in lines across the tablet, one line, then a space and another line, and another line until the entire tablet was filled. These he was sure contained the stories and the wisdom of the way of DOG and of DOG's only Puppy, NAV. But we cannot read them; perhaps our ancestors knew, but we do not. There are many of them, he said. Then he brought from his cardboard suitcase many sheets of paper. These, he said, they are made by frotando, rubbing across the tablets with crayons. The tiny paw prints stood out, clearly enough, though often smeared. I looked at them and at the tablet of gold with awe. The stories were true: they, the ancient ones, had placed tablets of gold throughout the world with the stories and wisdom of DOG.

And now this old man, wizened, had brought one for me to see, to know that they do exist, and with it the rubbings from the other tablets. These, he said, are all the writings we have. We hope they are all. We do not know. They have always been preserved as the Bark of DOG, and we cannot believe anyone would have lost or sold one.

He gave me the rubbings, the copies he had made, and begged me to decipher them, to read the strange script. I could not. I told him I could try, but it might take much time. It was only markings to me; I could not see the pattern in them. Stay with me, I said, tell me the stories and the wisdom of DOG that you know. But the old man shook his head sadly. Necesito regresar, I must return, they wait for me, they are afraid, and I tell them the stories and wisdom of DOG so we will be strong in our love and not hate those who would hurt us. They wait for me. I will leave with you the rubbings, the marks of the tablets. I will take with me the tableta de oro, it must be with the others, to take it away even this little time was hard, a great risk, so far from our home and the place where the others rest. I must bury it with the other tabletas, all the tabletas de oro together, so that the men with lust and hate and greed do not find them. I will leave with you these rubbings. They must be enough. Find the meaning in them. Then come to us with these stories, this wisdom that we may know and correct what we have been saying. Our words and the small dogs' barks are always a little different each time we tell the stories. We want to know the true Bark of DOG.

I was shaking. I could only nod, yes. Yes, I would try, it might take much time, but I will dedicate myself to understanding these marks, the paw prints. I begged him to stay and tell me the stories, I would drive him to the border, I would give him all, all I had, to him and to his fellow travelers in the way of DOG. But he shook his head, no. It is not for me, it is not for us. It is for the teaching of the way of love and peace that you must work. I must return the way I came, not with visa, not with papers, only my poor body across the Rio Grande. I have a little money, not much because I bought this suit when I arrived so I would not be ashamed in the presence of one who is holy to DOG. I nodded, filled with my mission, and said to him: Be never ashamed. Poverty is no shame, to be poor is no shame, there is no ceremony or glorious clothing we must wear. The only real poverty is the poverty of the heart that cannot love, the poverty of one who would grasp for power instead of sharing. You are rich, much richer than I. You know the stories, I said, you have the power of love. Perhaps as I learn to read the paw prints on the tabletas de oro I will become as strong in love and sharing as you.

I took him into the town where he said he would wait for the bus to El Paso. I gave him food, I tried to give him money, I stayed with him every moment I could, listening to what he said of his village and the followers of DOG. The bus came. "Vaya con dogos," he said. I took his hand and said, "Vaya con dogos." And he left.

It has been a great burden, a great calling to understand these tablets, to find the way to their meaning. I feel it every day, and I feel that I am not worthy. DOG, I am not worthy. But I persist. After eight years, alone on my small ranch, I finally was touched by DOG, he placed his paw upon me, the mark of his paw is there on my shoulder, always it will be there. And I was able to see. The prints are a script for Classic Sumerian, an ancient language. So ancient that these writings must come from more than 2,500 years ago; the gold does not tarnish. Studying that language, hour after hour, day after day, month after month, now four years, I have come to understand the paw prints. Slowly the meaning has emerged. And I have become stronger in the way of love, the way of peace that DOG's only Puppy, NAV, has taught us.

Now I have translations of the markings. I want to go to Mexico to find the old man and his village, to celebrate the stories and wisdom of DOG. But it is far, and I am old, and there is much danger. I have not heard from the old man since he left, and when I look at the satellite photos where the village should be I see only ruins, buildings aslant, and the fields look to be barren. I fear for them, though I know that if they have passed, then they have passed into the great flow of love of DOG and NAV and all others who have learned to love. Puede ser que se acabó el pueblo, pero no se acabó el amor.

Growing strong in the way of peace and love that DOG has given us, I have seen that my dogs are different with me. They play and bark with me, but they also seem closer, almost in awe. They have barked some message to me, and other dogs have come and smelled me and howled then jumped and danced with my dogs, circling me, playing, howling in some kind of joy. Those dogs leave, and others come, they smell me, howl and circle in a kind of ecstasy. One night I understood, DOG breathed in my ear, that I am now the DOGGY LAMA, the first human DOGGY LAMA. It is a great responsibility—not honor, for there is no honor to walk in the way of peace and love that DOG's only Puppy NAV teaches us. No honor, but the responsibility to live well, to be an example, and to teach.

I have translated as well as I can the paw prints, the strange markings that seem now to me as familiar as my hand. I understand them, I think, for I will never be sure. But this is what I have, and it is this I have written here. The rhythms, the rhymes of the Classic Sumerian I could not put into English. Each who translates must add his or her own voice, for me, the voice that DOG has given me. I put the writings in the order of the stories they tell. At the end of the chapter "The Birth of NAV" I have added a short paragraph of what the old man told me. And at the end of all I have put a little story called "The Animal Shelter" that I learned from my dogs and those who are near me. I have also included a report of a similar script for a prayer to NAV with the explanation of the provenance of that. But I have not been able to include a copy of the rubbings the old man brought to me. A year ago when I was gone from my ranch to get supplies, someone or something broke into the house. All that was taken, it seems, were those rubbings, the rubbings from the tabletas de oro—nothing else. I am not good with the computer, so I never made a scan of them. I kept them in a fireproof box, and I was certain my home was safe, no one had ever bothered it, far from other people at the end of a narrow dirt road. But they are lost, and in their place in the house, for many days, a lingering smell of cat, a smell I abhor.

I offer these writings, the stories and wisdom of the way of peace and love that DOG has given us through his only Puppy NAV. Read them slowly, no more than one on any day. Think. Then think with your heart. Practice the wisdom that we may live together in the flow of love.

In the Beginning

In the beginning was the Bark.

And the Bark was with DOG.

And the Bark was DOG.

There was the flow of all. No time, no change, no thing, only the great flow of all, swirling and forever, neither static nor moving, neither warm nor cold, neither full nor empty. The flow of all.

And in the flow of all came the Bark, and came DOG, the shape and form of the intelligence of love, the power of love, the thought of love to shape and form the flow of all.

And DOG barked. And from His bark, in the warmth of His breath, came the spirit and spirits of all, came many spirits not distinct, not separate, but parts of the flow of all, small swirlings in the great swirl of all, a vortex and another, a swirl that coalesced into spirit and intelligence. DOG who is the flow of all and is part of the flow of all breathed and barked the spirits of all within the flow, within the swirl of nothing and everything, within what was, what is neither static nor moving, neither warm nor cold, neither full nor empty, the flow of all. And there was time.

Then DOG barked again. And the spirits had form, shape more than the swirling within the swirling, yet never separate, still and always part of the flow of all, like a pond in the flow of a river, like a bay in the flow of the ocean, like a gust of wind in the flow of the air, the spirits had intelligence and form, but were part of all, never separate yet distinct, never distinct but real. They had form but not substance.

And the spirit and the spirits wished to be close to DOG. And DOG realized this and barked, "You are closer to me than you understand, for you are me and I am you and we are all together the flow of all. There is no close and far in the swirl of all. There is no better or worse. There is only the flow, and now shape and intelligence."

And DOG barked again. And the spirits who had form and shape, now could speak. They could speak and they spoke of their awe of DOG calling out, "Hallelujah!"

And DOG heard and He barked, "Cry not Hallelujah to me. Praise not me. I am only the spirit and breath of all that you are part of, I do not create but only recognize what is and what will be and what was. And as I recognize, as I see and understand, you become with form and speech. Praise not the Me, for I am the flow and you are the flow and we are all together. I speak and we all speak. The Bark makes us real but the Bark is us and we are the Bark, not separate and distinct."

Then DOG barked and His breath coalesced into stars.

Then DOG barked and His breath coalesced into the moon.

Then DOG barked and His breath coalesced into the earth.

And the earth was barren, rock and molten lava. So DOG raised His leg and cooled it with His water, and it had form and substance, land and water.

Then DOG barked again and the earth had life, had grass, had trees, had flowers and weeds, had moss and cactus. And the grass, the trees, the flowers and weeds, the moss and cactus were in shape and form and substance but were still part of all, part of the great flow and swirl, like a pond in the flow of a river, like a bay in the flow of the ocean, like a gust of wind in the flow of the air, real but not real, there only in the perception of those who would see and distinguish the parts of the flow of all.

But on the earth there was not intelligence, not understanding. So DOG called to the spirits of the swirl and flow of all and told them that some would go to earth, to populate it, to make a world of DOG, with variety beyond their imagining. And some would stay with Him, form only without substance.

Yes, some would go to the earth to realize intelligence. But not only intelligence, not only walking on the earth, or swimming in the sea, or flying in the air. They would realize love, for the swirl and flow of all was the spirit of DOG which is love, love that surpasseth understanding.

And the spirits were puzzled, they were confused. What is love? What is there but the flow of all and the Bark of DOG that shapes and forms? They knew not.

Then DOG barked that those who would go to the earth—some now, some millennia from now, some aeons from now—would live and die. And suffer. Yet always would they be part of Him and return to Him in His love. They would have to pass through life and death on earth in order to learn of love. Those who would stay, who would be part with him and not take substance on earth, they would be in the flow of love, but they would not know love, they would not be able to teach love nor to create love, but only live within love.

8   The BARK of DOG

Then all were filled with fear, lest they be chosen to go to earth and live and die and suffer. For they would not have pain because pain hurts.

Yet some were curious, were wanting, still intelligence without knowledge of love, they wanted to know of love. They were willing. And they came forward in thought to DOG.

And DOG chose some to be birds, some to be sheep, some to be horses, some to be rattlesnakes, some to be fish, some to be bears, some to be monkeys, and from the monkey would come later the bigger monkeys, then apes, and finally men and women, humans who would be born in love and would understand above all others. And there were those He graced by making into creatures in His own image, into dogs who would carry the giving of love in their every breath, dogs who would be the embodiment of love to teach the humans to understand and to love.

Then the spirit and form CAT purred to DOG. She would help, she mewed, and DOG saw that CAT was intelligent and capable. So she helped, always at DOG's will, learning, giving form and substance to one spirit as a fish, to another as an eel, to another as a boa constrictor. And she was filled with pride, for she could create. She had pride. Then she had allegiance to no one, not even DOG. And she created a creature in her own image, did CAT, a mountain lion, and she called him FERRATSI.

And DOG barked to CAT that she should return to His spirit, that she, too, could learn to love. But CAT would create, she had power, and she cajoled some who were willing to be born to live and die and suffer so that they should love, she cajoled them to come to her and be formed for the earth in her image. To be hers there on earth. They came, for they knew not love, but had only hope. Nor did CAT know love, but only power.

And DOG barked to her again to follow the way of DOG, the way of love, to learn to be at peace. And CAT would not listen, for she was filled with pride, and she would create, for she had power.

DOG tried once more to bring CAT to him. He barked. But she would not heed, she mewed but did not turn in her thought. She created more in her image.

Then DOG said, "You do not love, you do not recognize the way of peace and love and being all together. So you shall be our tool, our tool in your ignorance, you will take to those who have form and substance and intelligence the challenges of fear and hate, of vengeance and sloth, of guilt and schadenfreude, of greed and lust, of gluttony and impatience, of indifference and pride, and of allergy. You shall take all these horrors that can infest the spirit to those who have form and substance and intelligence on earth. For only with these horrors as challenges shall they learn to recognize love, to have a loving heart. You shall live always between the swirl of spirit and form without substance and the earth, in a kind of void, dark, but able to see and to test my creatures who would learn to love."

Then DOG threw CAT out of heaven for her pride.

And CAT fell and fell and fell, through the void and darkness she fell, falling with no weight, yet falling, and she grasped with her claws at a ridge, a place that DOG had allotted her, high above the earth. She grasped and pulled herself up, for now she had substance. Her fur on end, she sat and looked. Then she began to preen herself, to lick her paws and then her fur, to be beautiful as she knew she was beautiful. And she mewed, and she mewed again, and some who were far from DOG heard her. And they came to see, and she purred to them, "I shall make you great. You shall live but never die, you shall live but not suffer. You shall live and have only pleasure." And they were seduced and agreed to go to earth to be her minions. First came FERRATSI, the great mountain lion, powerful, who would not die but work forever for her, to show the power of CAT, CAT, the only one of the spirits who would challenge DOG. Then came the others, the ones who would live forever on earth, not suffering but always pleasuring themselves as cats, the twelve cats of CAT. And CAT gave substance to HATE, to GREED, to VENGEANCE, to LUST, to GLUTTONY, to PRIDE, to IMPATIENCE, to INDIFFERENCE, to SLOTH, to SCHADENFREUDE, to GUILT, and to ALLERGY. Above them all she placed FEAR who would, under the always stern guidance of FERRATSI, lead these twelve cats of CAT to turn all on earth away from DOG.

And DOG did not interfere. He saw, and He knew that this was necessary. "You, too, are part of My plan, for there can be no true loving-kindness if there are not the challenges of these cats to those who will be born and die. These cats, though they be horrible, still are they part of Me, part of My plan." And He barked to them, "Should you some day repent, should you some day come to realize the love that transcends all, that is greater than death, should you some day have a loving heart, then you shall return to my side. For though ye be far

from me, even the most despicable of spirits can return to my love if they will."
And the cats preened themselves, INDIFFERENCE already powerful.

So HATE, GREED, VENGEANCE, LUST, GLUTTONY, PRIDE, IMPATIENCE, INDIFFERENCE, SLOTH, SCHADENFREUDE, GUILT, and ALLERGY, led by FEAR, who answered only to FERRATSI, who answered only to CAT, descended onto the earth. There they spawned many little cats that kill and kill and kill, torturing mice and birds, finding pleasure in the suffering of others, filled with pride because of their power to hurt.

And DOG saw that the mice and birds would not survive to learn to love. The many cats could hear the mice, could hear with their sharp ears how the mice talked with clicks. So He taught the mice to click more softly, such quiet mouse-clicks. And to the birds with feathers DOG gave the ability to fly, to fly into the trees so that some would live, that cats would not kill them.

DOG put many upon the earth. The mice, the birds, the trees, the rabbits, so many in a variety that none but He could comprehend. And dogs, too, in His image, He placed on earth. And among those He placed were many creatures who could think and learn. He waited, then, to see which would learn to love. For the spirit of love cannot be forced, it can only be learned, the great flow of all enriched by the intelligences that become guided by love. Only through suffering can any creature know deeply the power of love. And DOG saw that this is the best of all possible worlds, though suffering and pain abound from the spirit of CAT. For this is the world that will come to love, love that is more powerful than death, love that is the swirl and flow of all.

The Birth of NAV,
the Only Puppy of DOG

Sunset in the desert. The Winter Solstice. Rosy-fingered sunset over the mountains. Maria, a poor young peasant girl, pushed out from her family and village to live alone in the desert, mistaking her good heart for wantonness. Maria, who loves but does not lust, who holds dear and who would be an example for those who could see, mistaken, alone in a small hut in the desert, bereft. She stands outside the door of her hut, gazing at the sunset, filled with love for all creatures, and there is a FLASH OF LIGHT. Sudden, brilliant, blinding—averting her eyes, she sees at her feet a Puppy, NAV the only Puppy of DOG, sent by DOG to bring love, and hope, and, faithfulness, and loyalty, and courage to all. A small, whimpering Puppy, only a small bundle of fur, squirming, eyes not yet open, whining, with an umbilical cord going up, up, up to Heaven. Maria is filled with love, and in the sunset she touches the umbilical cord which turns to gold dust, falling into a pile at her feet. Bewildered, she kneels and picks up NAV. He whimpers—arfy, arfy—and she presses him close to her, comforting him in the gathering dusk. Always when he needs help from Maria will he cry "arfy, arfy," and so we, too, when we ask that Santa Maria the foster-mother of NAV may give us help, we pray ARFY MARIA. And Maria gathers the few twigs and branches she has saved and builds a small fire, knowing it will last no more than a little while, but enough to warm her and NAV in the growing darkness and growing cold of the desert.

Then from the dark, in the last light of day, come the animals of the forest and desert, drawn by the scent of NAV. Howling, with joy and confusion, the wolf comes near to the circle of light of the fire next to the buffalo, who lowing, salutes and recognizes the love of NAV. And the coyote nuzzles next to the rabbit, yipping with joy, the donkey and the bear draw close, the quail and all the birds of the desert, all come and lie down together in peace in the light of NAV, in the smell of Him who brings peace and love. And the fire continues to burn, warm and glowing though the branches and twigs are not consumed. The wolf, the buffalo, the coyote, the rabbit, the donkey, the bear, the birds, they all rest, sniffing, rustling slightly, soft in the peace of NAV.

When comes out of the darkness, in the distance, a high shriek from the desert. FERRATSI, the mountain lion, sent by CAT, by CAT whom DOG threw out of heaven for her pride. FERRATSI shrieks again, and gathers to her then the twelve cats of CAT, who are called HATE, GREED, VENGEANCE, LUST, FEAR, GLUTTONY, PRIDE, IMPATIENCE, INDIFFERENCE, SLOTH, SCHADENFREUDE, GUILT, and ALLERGY. Come they down on the fold, down on those at peace in the light of NAV, scattering the wolf, the buffalo, the coyote, the rabbit, the donkey, the bear, the birds, all flee before FERRATSI and her cats. But these emissaries, these minions of CAT come not to hunt for meat, nor to slaughter these innocents, but to destroy NAV—to keep the peace and love of DOG from all, from those who want to learn to love and be faithful, to be kind and courageous, to keep all this from DOG's creatures come the twelve cats of CAT to destroy NAV, to tear apart Maria. They gather at the edge of the light, the fire still burning warmly, ready to pounce, licking their whiskers, waiting only for the command of FERRATSI, who pads up slowly, growling, swiping at the air with her great paw, claws extended.

Maria, with NAV in her arms, stands ready to fight them all, fearless in the love of NAV, in the courage of DOG who fills her with strength. Then NAV, small and newborn, opens his eyes, and sees, and smells, and jumps from her arms and stands before her. And facing FERRATSI and the twelve cats of CAT—He stares at them, and they turn their eyes away, yes, even FERRATSI cannot meet His eyes. And NAV yips, twice, lunging only a little towards them. And they scatter into the night, in fear, each in his own direction with only FERRATSI giving a last shriek as she bounds away by herself far, far from the light of NAV. FERRATSI turns in hatred, planning, going out to find many cats who will insinuate themselves into the homes of those whom they would destroy by leading them to FERRATSI, who follows only CAT.

Then NAV turns to Maria, closing his eyes, whimpering, arfy, arfy, and Maria, the foster-mother of NAV, picks him up and sits with him in the light of the fire where are the gifts that the animals of the forest and desert have left, food enough for many days, as there will be food always for Maria and NAV from the animals of the forest and desert who have learned love from NAV.

Thus was born NAV, Dog's only Puppy, who lived and suffered so that we might know love and peace. Many now follow Him and through him DOG who smells all we do.

* * * * * * * * * * *

Yet we remain hidden, avoiding persecution from the followers of CAT, hidden from the hate of those who do not know the love of NAV. But we keep the faith, we are a light to all people, and still we sing now at the Winter Solstice our song of joy, that song from the Mayan believers: FELIZ NAV Y DOG.

Joy, for the birth of NAV, the only Puppy of DOG.

The Ascension into Heaven of NAV, DOG's Only Puppy

The Winter Solstice and NAV, Dog's only puppy, on his 910th birthday, begins his final journey.

For many dog-years NAV had not run, had not jumped, had not played and gamboled. He had spent his years teaching, teaching always with joy. He had no puppies, He had no mate, only teaching, for His compassion to all was great.

There by the Euphrates, NAV barked, then barked again. And came Juney, the sweet, the peaceful, the joyful, from the oasis of Kelev Tov near the Dead Sea. Hearing the call of NAV she came, she licked Nav's face, and laid down beside Him.

Then came Bidú, the great protector, padding happily with eagerness, black and white fur flying wildly, giant that he was, with his square face, his huge head, powerful shoulders, ready to come, to learn, to give, came he from the North, from the cold of the steppes, came he to NAV. Hearing the call of NAV he came, he licked Nav's face, and laid down beside Him.

Came also Paw, the gruff, the surly who hid his great heart behind his black, black short coat, big, trotting almost sideways, from the fertile ground near the Ganges, a cigar in his mouth, drooling, sniffing. Hearing the call of NAV he came, he licked Nav's face, and laid down beside Him.

Then appeared Spot, all white with a black spot on his brow, short hair, jumping and jumping, ready always to spring against CAT, who sends her twelve cats and FERRATSI the mountain lion. Spot always ready, alert but happy, came he from the mountains and cedars of Lebanon. Hearing the call of NAV he came, he licked Nav's face, and laid down beside Him.

With joy came Sultan, the puppy of Spot, the second generation of those who would follow DOG through NAV, perplexed, yet unsteady, sniffing, curious, not yet full of wisdom, yet full of joy and love, came he from the Red Sea, from the desert. Hearing the call of NAV he came, he licked NAV's face, and laid down beside Him.

Came also Ralph, with his purple coat, his look aslant and always joking, always wry and teaching through his jabs, through the laughter, he walked slowly, for he, too, was old, the first of the followers of DOG through NAV. From the woods near the Aral Sea where he taught the love that passes all understanding, hearing the call of NAV he came, he licked Nav's face, and laid down beside Him.

Then came Lady, old too, regal, white and golden her hair flowing out, her tail straight out, knowing that the bark of NAV was her call to come, to journey to the side of her master in love. Came Lady from the land of olives, a small village called Catulus on the Middle Sea, she came, she licked Nav's face, and laid down beside Him.

And Birta came, very, very old, brown and black, almost deaf, walking so slowly, looking and looking, for she had heard the great call of NAV, and though her journey was almost over, though she had led the people to love for many years, she rejoiced to hear the call of NAV, to know she would be at his side once more. Came Birta from the cold mountains on the Caspian Sea, hearing the call of NAV she came, she licked Nav's face, and laid down beside Him.

Came, too, Prometheus, the bold, the strong, so tall, so strong, with massive jaws, full of life, short tan hair, large paws, came he from the cold north of the Baltic Sea, from the forests and streams, flowing steady in his run, not fast nor slow, but continuous, focused on reaching NAV he came, he licked Nav's face, and laid down beside Him.

And Fido came, the faithful one, small, with curling tail, black and white and tan and red, all intense, came Fido from near on the Euphrates, for though he taught, he had always to be near NAV, he had never learned to carry NAV in his heart and not yearn always to be near Him. Hearing the call of NAV he came, he licked Nav's face, and laid down beside Him.

Princess, too, came, the lovely one, shaggy and black and horrible to look at until you saw her eyes and the love that flowed from them, her rat-like tail wagging her greeting as she came from the foothills of the Hindu Kush. She came, she licked Nav's face, and laid down beside Him.

And Feral, the wild one, unkempt, with head too big and paws too small, came he from the wild places in India, from the forests of the big cats and large elephants. Hearing the call of NAV he came, he licked Nav's face, and laid down beside Him.

Came thus the twelve disciples of NAV, they came, those whom He had taught of love, of the love that goes beyond needing, of the love that goes beyond compassion, of the love that goes to the heart, wanting nothing in return but the chance to love. Juney, Bidú, Paw, Spot, Sultan, Ralph, Lady, Birta, Prometheus, Fido, Princess, and Feral had gone out from Him, one at a time, as they had learned the love beyond comprehending, to lead humans to accept love as the first step to giving love. They had gone, too, to the old ones, the ones with sloped foreheads, so like the humans yet shorter, squat, more massive. But the slope-heads had not been able to learn, they had thrown stones at Fido, and Sultan now limped from the branch that a slope-head had used to hit his leg. No, the slope-heads could not learn, they could not accept the way of DOG, and so they would not continue. They were strong but their strength was not from love, they were smart, but they were not wise with the wisdom of DOG.

But the humans, they had accepted the love that NAV led them to. Slowly, they became less wild, gathering together, learning to trust, hunting with the aid of Juney and Spot, kept warm at night nestled against Birta, touching and being touched, the humans became domesticated. Juney, Bidú, Paw, Spot, Sultan, Ralph, Lady, Birta, Prometheus, Fido, Princess, and Feral each carried the message of unconditional love to them, to one human, then to a group, and finally when the humans collected together protected by the followers of NAV and their puppies in small villages. Humans became more than animals that had to eat and breed, they became people who could love and trust and care for one another, who would not abandon their sick, who would care until the very end, who would fight and sacrifice themselves for the weakest among them. Compassion, needing, trust, these they learned from Juney, Bidú, Paw, Spot, Sultan, Ralph, Lady, Birta, Prometheus, Fido, Princess, and Feral. But from NAV they learned love, unconditional love, and became PEOPLE of DOG.

Then DOG saw that it was good, that people could follow His Way, and He had pity on the humans, for they had no tails to wag, nor could they bark. So He let NAV send Juney to teach them to speak. And they learned to talk, and they learned to sing, and they sang the praises of NAV. Then NAV grew sad and told Juney to go to them and tell them to sing only of DOG, for DOG is the father of all, NAV only his Puppy given to the world to teach of love.

And DOG saw that it was good, that people could follow his Way, and He had pity on them, for He had given them no fur, they huddled together in caves in warm places. So He let NAV send Prometheus to teach them of fire, of how to build a fire, of how to carry a fire, of how to make the singing sticks of fire. And Prometheus, with great joy in his heart, took fire to humans, so humans could gather at night to talk, to sit and pet a dog, to tell one another of peace and love, so humans could invite others to come to their fire and warm themselves and cook their food. And with the gifts of speech and fire the humans became more people, more than animals, more able to love and nurture. Then went the humans to colder places, and with them went Bidú and Ralph and Birta and their puppies, yes their puppies unto the thirteenth generation, kept warm, too, by the fires the humans would build.

Now at the end of his 910th year, NAV called them all, his twelve disciples, to begin his final journey. They came from all the places where they had been with humans, teaching humans unconditional love and trust, they came from the humans they had grown to love and trust. Sadly they left them, they left also their mates and puppies, left them, yet came with joy to answer the bark of NAV.

Slowly NAV began to walk, steadily, not fast nor slow, steadily, going to the East and to the North, crossing desert and river and forest, leading the twelve disciples from the Euphrates to the mountains. Weak but strong in His purpose He led, with Juney and Bidú tending always to Him, at his side should He stumble. And Fido, always close to NAV, almost underfoot, licking Him and trying to help Juney and Bidú. And Sultan walking alongside Birta to help her, with Prometheus at the side of Lady, who, though old, continued apace. They walked and walked, looking ahead, and Princess walking at the side. Spot ranging in front, in back, here and there, with Bidú always aware too, careful always that the twelve cats of CAT led by FERRATSI should not hinder them. And Paw, gruff and growling came he with Ralph at his side, but not joking, no, no simple talk, for they all knew that this was the last journey of NAV. And at the back, at the end, always a little behind the others, came Feral, looking to the left, to the right, behind, but not ahead.

Slowly, weak though strong in purpose, NAV placed one paw in front of another and led them, upright, panting only slightly as He continued. Each night they stopped to rest, eating what Prometheus or Princess would bring, for they were the good hunters, the ones who would provide, though all tried, for they all cared. They shared, and this, too, they had taught to the humans. Sharing to bring each closer. And NAV looked on, eating only a little, for He knew that He needed His strength only for a little more to complete His journey.

Then they came to the northern part of the river Indus, came they in Spring when all was flowering. The twelve disciples entered the cold, cold deep fast-flowing waters and placed themselves one next to another so that NAV could cross by stepping on their backs, not getting his paws wet. But NAV barked, and they came back to Him, and He barked again, and the waters parted. He looked only straight ahead, and they crossed the deep fast-flowing waters on dry ground.

They passed then the wild forests, thick and black near the mountains, and they heard the wolves, howling, long and mournful howling, and NAV was sad. For the wolves howled because they could not learn the love of DOG, they could not learn to trust and to care and to share with any but their own. Wild they were, and though kin, they could only howl but come no closer to DOG. And NAV was sad, but He continued on, for He had tried to teach them and had only scars now where they had not learned.

As they passed then through the desert they heard chanting in the distance. Passing closer they found forty-two humans chanting, beating a drum, repeating over and over:

> Hairy doggy, hairy doggy,
> Doggy doggy, hairy hairy.
> Hairy mama, hairy mama,
> Mama mama, hairy hairy.

They chanted to reach the Doghead. NAV would not stop, He passed with sadness and compassion for these who search for only faith and meditation, not the practices that lead to love and caring and sharing with all. But his journey must continue, and passing on they heard the chant receding:

> Hairy doggy, hairy doggy,
> Doggy doggy, hairy hairy.
> Hairy mama, hairy mama,
> Mama mama, hairy hairy.

> Hairy doggy, hairy doggy,
> Doggy doggy, hairy hairy.
> Hairy mama, hairy mama,
> Mama mama, hairy hairy

> Hairy doggy, hairy doggy,
> Doggy doggy, hairy hairy.
> Hairy mama, hairy mama,
> Mama mama, hairy hairy.

And they came to a land of great palms, of sand and lush forest, of grass leading to a knoll, and they heard the sound of the sea. As they reached the top of the knoll, they saw the ocean at the great Bay of Bengal, slowly lapping in waves

The Ascension into Heaven   21

to the beach of pure sand. Then NAV rested, lying down, placing his head on his paws, and He gave a great sigh. There, under the bodhi tree, next to the clear spring called Jabu, He closed His eyes, breathing steadily, deeply meditating. He was weak but his spirit was strong with wisdom.

On the third day, a rabbit, a very small rabbit with a round, fluffy, white tail, was filled with the love of NAV and with awe of this great moment, and she hopped to NAV. She twitched her whiskers near to Him, and offered herself that He may eat and not become weak. She offered herself with love and awe. And NAV roused His head and He licked her, gazing at her with compassion and love, and with His muzzle pushed her away, letting her know that her offer was great, but He had no need for food on this His last day. And the bunny hopped off, filled with His love and with joy, for she had been one with Him for a moment, and the twelve disciples did not molest her for they saw that she was good.

Then NAV roused his head and called to the twelve. He called to them, and they came, from the oldest to the youngest.

First came Ralph, who smelled Him and licked His face, and NAV smelled him, standing weakly but strong in His wisdom, and licked his face.

Then came Birta, who smelled Him and licked His face, and NAV smelled her, standing weakly but strong in His wisdom, and licked her face.

Then came Lady, who smelled Him and licked His face, and NAV smelled her, standing weakly but strong in His wisdom, and licked her face.

Then came Paw, who smelled Him and licked his face, and NAV smelled him, standing weakly but strong in His wisdom, and licked his face.

Then came Juney, who smelled Him and licked his face, and NAV smelled her, standing weakly but strong in His wisdom, and licked her face.

Then came Prometheus, who smelled Him and licked His face, and NAV smelled him, standing weakly but strong in His wisdom, and licked his face.

Then came Bidú, who smelled Him and licked His face, and NAV smelled him, standing weakly but strong in His wisdom, and licked his face.

Then came Spot, who smelled Him and licked His face, and NAV smelled him, standing weakly but strong in His wisdom, and licked his face.

Then came Fido, who smelled Him and licked His face, and NAV smelled him, standing weakly but strong in His wisdom, and licked his face.

Then came Princess, who smelled Him and licked His face, and NAV smelled her, standing weakly but strong in His wisdom, and licked her face.

Then came Sultan, who smelled Him and licked His face, and NAV smelled him, standing weakly but strong in His wisdom, and licked his face.

Then came Feral, almost cringing, not the youngest but the last, and he smelled NAV and hesitantly licked His face, and NAV smelled him and licked his face.

They all smelled Him and were smelled by Him. Each licked Him and was licked by Him. Then they began to howl with anguish. And NAV barked softly and they stopped. He told them that there was no cause for anguish, for sorrow. And Sultan spoke and said they would be lost without Him, they could see He was going, and there was no one to replace Him, no one but He and His love who could guide them. And NAV was near to angry, but calm with compassion He remembered how Sultan was young, and He barked softly. Had they not learned that whoever carries the Bark of DOG in his heart, who could bring love and joy to others, was near to NAV? Wherever there are two of you, or three, or even just one, there will I be, NAV told them. And I do not die, nor will you die, but we continue on, forever, part of the process of all, enriching the great flow of love with our part of compassion and love and caring. And they wagged their tails, did Juney, Bidú, Paw, Spot, Sultan, Ralph, Lady, Birta, Prometheus, Fido, Princess, and Feral.

Then NAV got up, slowly He padded toward the sea until He was only a little way from the waves that lapped on the beach. The clear day, sun brightly shining, was waning. He turned to his disciples and told them that they would find among them one who would be tasked to teach, to carry through caring all who would love, who would carry the wisdom. And she stepped forward, did Juney, for she knew it was she that NAV meant, and NAV went to her and placed his paw on her heart, and barked "Arf, arf, arf, arf, arf." And she, Juney, the one who had never put herself forward, who had learned and cared for others, she was the first DOGGY LAMA. Then NAV said that there would always be a DOGGY LAMA, that when one passed into the flow of all, the flow of love, another would be found, not a re-incarnation of spirit or body, but a re-incarnation of love, and in each generation they would seek out him or her, smelling the crotch of each until they found the chosen one. And one day, NAV said, they would find a human who will have learned the love of all, the caring and unconditional love, and he shall be called Arf, the PROPHET of DOG, and be the first human DOGGY LAMA. But never a re-incarnation, no, no passing of spirit or body but a direct line of love. It is not blood that carries the message of love, for we are all equal, said NAV, in our ability to care and love, from the weakest to the strongest, from the smartest to the dumbest. Nay, I hold close to me those who are born with heads too big, who cannot learn, who remain always children, for they carry more than any the spirit of love and trust and caring.

And then He said, in a bark so low and sad they could barely hear: There is one among you who will betray our love, who will follow the way of CAT, and you shall know that one when that dog who would be cat, who would have the pleasures that are transitory rather than love, claims to be closer to me than all. Then shall you know that the division is the work of CAT who has misled that one through FERRATSI the mountain lion. But grieve not, for those who are misled, who have lost the way of peace, can be brought back through love and teaching. And they looked one at the other, but saw no sign, and they licked one another, for whatever would be they were sisters and brothers in the love of DOG through NAV.

Then NAV looked out over the sea, and He looked up to the sky as the sun began to set behind the knoll, rosy-fingered sunset, as the full moon began to rise in the East, and the sky slowly turned from bright blue and yellow to muted colors. He barked that they should celebrate the next day, not mourn but organize, for they are the chosen ones, and their mission is to help more and more become chosen ones, until all know the message of compassion, of caring, of love. And He laid down on the beach, the waves all calm, and gave one long howl, "Aroooo," and said—not to the twelve but more to himself—"Father I come to Thee." And He placed His head on His paws and slowly began to rise. Then Juney, Bidú, Paw, Spot, Sultan, Ralph, Lady, Birta, Prometheus, Fido, Princess, and Feral all watched, all attentive, sitting, looking on as NAV lying with his head on his paws rises slowly into the clear sky, into the sunset, into the light of the full moon, slowly higher and higher, rising always until He could be seen no more and only a faint sigh came to them from the sky, from the light of the stars in the dark sky, "Peace, I sit at the right paw of DOG. Peace and love shall be thy way, kindness and attentiveness. I am with you always."

No thunder, no crashing of waves, no lightning, but only the warm, sweet air and calm sea. Only peace. And the twelve all howled one long howl, "Arooooo," and yipped. And then they frolicked, yes, jumped and nipped each other, for they knew that there was no death but only the process of all enriched by each in his love, in her love, and that love was joy, and playful, and tails wagging.

Then they laid down in the dark, lying close one to another, snuffling a little, meditating much, coughing or a twitch of a leg. And on the next morning, as rosy-fingered dawn came above the bay to the East, they were hungry, and they wished to celebrate, for NAV had not died but only passed to the right paw of DOG and given them their mission. They looked, and they heard a great wave coming from the ocean, and there as it receded, they saw upon the beach oysters and oysters and oysters. But they knew not what to do with them, they were bewildered, for they could find no way to open them. Then came Juney and said, "Arf arf arf": The spirit of DOG through NAV is sufficient. And they gathered the oysters into a great mound, and they sat around the heap of oysters, and they closed their eyes in meditation, and in an instant, there, the oysters opened, not one, not two, but all of them. And they ate of the oysters and were happy. This on the first full moon after the Spring Equinox of the 911th year of NAV.

And so each year on the first full moon of the Spring Equinox we celebrate the Ascension into Heaven of NAV, Dog's Only Puppy, at the festival of Oyster. And when we celebrate Oyster we honor with joy the rabbit who would offer herself as sacrifice through love, we remember her by giving to our dearest sweets to eat, saying they are in honor of the Oyster Bunny.

The Preaching of St. Paw to the Gangesians

Do you believe?

Do you believe?

Do you believe in DOG?

The one and only who sits on His throne in heaven.

And sees all we do. And scents all we do.

And I say thank Dogness, yes thank Dogness for that. For He shall protect us from our enemies, nay even from ourselves shall He protect us.

It is He who has enjoined us to cleanliness, for cleanliness is next to Doglieness.

Yes clean. And He does not say, "Clean mind, clean body." No, He knows, that DOG who smells all we do, that the world is too muddy, too dusty, the fleas too ferocious for us to keep our coats immaculate.

But our minds, our minds can be clean, free of all temptation, chastising His enemies.

My fellow dogs—some of you have fallen into error, into uncleanness, have followed Satan, that vile cat whose name is JEZEBEL; thinking it is merely fun, to feed her idolatrous images on earth, to make paintings, calendars with her features. Let me say that DOG abhors this, for He abhors CAT. It is the way of sin, of temptation, of temptation yielded to. It is a perversion of all that is Dogly in the world. It smells, it stinks, it reeks of cattiness to the very steps of heaven. Of heaven, where DOG has thrown out CAT for her pride. For her pride.

Yes, that Great German Shepherd who will treat us kindly if we but follow His will, enjoins us to love all that is Dogly and put from us all that is evil and catty.

But are there among us some who say that they are Dogly, yet worship a collie? Say that Lassie reigns upon the throne of heaven? Foul! Foul heresy! Foul heresy I say! Neither Lassie, nor a terrier, nor a great dane rules us all; neither a labrador, nor a spaniel, nor a poodle cares about our every action. Only DOG, who is a German Shepherd, will provide us with bones, with steaks, with a warm place to sleep.

Now some of you, some of you wish to be saved. I say you wish to be saved, but know not how. You eat and sleep, and act in a Dogly fashion, but DOG is not in you, He is not in your heart. Nay, you love Him not, nor fear Him rightly, but act Dogly from fear of the pack or ignorance only.

Only, only, on a rare, moonlit night, when all is still, and your heart is open to all nature, only then, sometimes, does the scent in the wind remind you that you are not alone, that DOG watches over you, and loves you, and will come if you call. Yes, He will come, with love, licking your soul, nuzzling up to your heart, if you but call. Do you believe? Do you believe? Do you believe in DOG?

Then let DOG hear you!

Let DOG hear you! Arrrooooo! Arrrooooo!

DOG I am not worthy! Arrrooooo! Arrrooooo! Hallelujah, Arrrooooo!

Join me my dogs, my fellows, in praise to DOG. Arrrooooo! Will you not come forward! Will you not come forward??

Well, let it be. DOG's spirit cannot be forced. Some day you shall feel His paw upon your heart. And rejoice.

Until that day, dogren, let DOG know that you care, that you wish for the day when heaven will be on earth, when all praise DOG, and Satan, the cat, shall no longer be seen; let DOG know. I say, let Him know by helping His servants. Here. Yes, your humble servant; help DOG by giving, give as you can, open your trove of bones if not your heart. I will be coming round you in a moment, yes around you. Give, give until your very hackles stir, that DOG's will may be done.

Praise DOG!

The Death of Juney

After the Ascension of NAV, DOG's only Puppy, the twelve disciples of NAV returned to their homes, to their mates and puppies, to the humans they were teaching of love.

Juney, now the DOGGY LAMA, went back to Kelev Tov near the Dead Sea. She found there the humans lost in their way, unsure, smelling of decay and fear. She showed them love, she went to the sick and licked their feet, she licked even the sores of the lepers. She wagged her tail, letting the humans touch her, petting her in the hope of learning the lessons of love from her. And they grew strong in the lessons of love.

She traveled then, for she had so much to give. To the Euphrates, where she gave hope to Fido, so bereft since the Ascension of NAV, looking always for Him, always lonely, always unsure. Juney barked to Fido to be of good spirit, that NAV was with them when they were together in the faith of Him and of DOG the Father. She barked as she trotted away that Fido should be of good cheer, teaching love and caring through his example always.

And Juney traveled to the cold steppes of the North to join with Bidú, the great protector, bringing care and help to the humans who had taken fire with them to the freezing, the fire that Prometheus had brought them, to settle there in the cold winds. Together Juney and Bidú taught the humans to hunt reindeer, to find yaks and horses to help them. And the yaks and horses went willingly with the humans when Juney told them of NAV and the Bark of DOG.

Traveled then did Juney to the cold of the Baltic Sea to find Prometheus. But there she found only wolves and savage humans, covered with hair, unclean and uncaring; Prometheus had died. Yes, Prometheus, the bold, so tall, so strong, with massive jaws, full of life, short tan hair, large paws, had grown old, had been less vigilant. And CAT saw that he was not strong, that the humans did not protect him but only wanted from him, and she sent FERRATSI the mountain lion and the twelve cats of CAT. Yes, FERRATSI brought with her HATE, GREED, VENGEANCE, LUST, FEAR, GLUTTONY, PRIDE, IMPATIENCE, INDIFFERENCE, SLOTH, SCHADENFREUDE, GUILT, and ALLERGY. Prometheus in his sleep smelled danger, but his sleep was deep, the sleep of the just, and he did not wake until the twelve cats of CAT set upon him, tearing him. He woke and snapped at them, but they were too fast, and he too weak, too old, his massive jaws closing only on air as they tore him, as they rendered his flesh, until, with his last breath he bellowed "BLESSED BE DOG AND HIS ONLY

PUPPY THAT I AM GRATEFUL FOR THE LIFE YOU HAVE GIVEN ME. FATHER, NAV, I come to thee." And he died, and there, in the cold, in the hard rock and frost near the frozen sea, his blood soaked into the ground. And a tree grew, a great spruce, the only spruce, the only tree for as far as a dog could travel in two days. The holy spruce grew as the twelve cats of CAT retired, licking their whiskers and paws, mewing with satisfaction, returning to FERRATSI, sated, glinting. For they had killed the bringer of fire, the great friend and guardian of humans, and the humans were afraid. They knew not what to do. They feared, and they carved from a great block of wood a statue of CAT to worship, certain that her power was great. They worshipped. Until Juney came. Then Juney was sad, not angry for that would be a sign of the power of CAT, for it is CAT who teaches only anger, fear, hurt, power. Juney went up to the woman Brigitta and nuzzled to her and licked her face. She went up to the man Jocko, and she nuzzled to him and licked his face. She went to their children, curling next to them that they could pet her and play with her. And Juney was happy, jumping and running, chasing and being chased so that the children knew for the first time since the death of Prometheus the power of love and joy. And Brigitta and Jocko, too, they smiled, and they learned, as Juney stayed with them, to love and to care, and they brought other humans to their fire and camp. And they were sore ashamed that they had not protected Prometheus. But he was gone, said Juney, he could not be here, and they had known the power and horror of CAT through her chosen one FERRATSI. The humans felt guilt, and Juney led them to see that GUILT was another of the cats of FERRATSI, that only joy, the joy of the love that DOG through NAV teaches could redeem them. Joy, but not forgetting. For regret, she told them, is the paralysis of hope.

And the humans took the big carved cat they had worshipped, and they put it into the fire. Then there was a shriek, a cry of great sound and power from the forest, as FERRATSI grew cold from the burning, as FERRATSI saw her power over these humans, the power of fear and hatred, burn into the sky. And Juney led them all in a dance, dancing and chasing around the fire, and they ate of rabbits they had found, for the rabbits multiplied so well and the bunnies remembered their bond with the followers of NAV from the time of the great mother rabbit, the one who had offered herself to NAV.

Then Juney went on, not afraid of FERRATSI and the twelve cats of CAT, for she was strong in the faith of NAV, and aware, and would not succumb. And the twelve cats of CAT fled before her, fled, as FERRATSI called to them to look for others to convert to the faith of CAT.

Juney then went to the Caspian Sea to find Birta. For Juney was old, and she knew it was time to say the last farewells to those who had travelled with NAV in the path of DOG. But there she could not find Birta. Birta, who had loved and been loved, who had cared, the humans said that she was old, so old, her brown and black now all grey, crippled with pain in her shoulders, Birta had come to them that they may pet her one final time, to lick each of them, and then slowly crawled to the forest, growling and barking when they tried to follow, went she to the forest alone. And there, unnoticed, alone, she died, she breathed once more, and with her last breath barked, "FATHER, NAV, I come to thee in the faith and hope of love." And Juney went to the forest, for the humans could not find the last place of Birta, and Juney smelled and Juney smelled and Juney smelled until she found the odor of Birta mixed with a sweet smell, a wisp of the odor that she had known only when NAV had ascended to heaven. And Juney squatted and marked the spot, marked it with her water, and the humans who had followed rejoiced, not sad but glad. And Juney led them to a great stone, so great that twenty humans could not lift it. And they labored, labored in the love and memory of Birta to move the stone. No writing on it—for they knew not how to write—just the great stone that took the humans two days and two nights to move to where Birta had breathed last.

Juney went on, taking everywhere with her the message of love. Then came she to the humans not far from the Ganges, who were chanting still, "Hairy Doggy, Hairy Doggy, Doggy Doggy, Hairy Hairy, . . .". They had learned of the power of DOG, yet they had not attended to NAV when He passed by them; they would attain to the Doghead through perfect faith, through chanting and meditation. And Juney was sad. She laid down near them, half-crazed from the sound of their chanting. And then she stood, powerful, with hackles raised, and she barked the Bark of DOG.

> There are three things. These three: Faith, Hope, and Charity.
> And of these three the greatest is Charity.

And the humans, shaggy and covered in sweat, stopped, they listened to the Bark of DOG. And Juney explained, in yips and growls and barks, that DOG cares not for faith, cares not for unity with those who would not bring love and charity to those they meet. Only the deeds, the action of love, the deep loving and caring can bring one close to NAV and through Him to DOG. And Juney barked the Bark of DOG:

> Never pass up an opportunity to be generous.

And she jumped, did Juney, jumped and spun, though she was old, cavorted, for she, too, loved to dance and play. And the humans, the Hairy Doggies, they smiled, and they laughed, and slowly, they began to learn from Juney. This final Bark of DOG they kept sacred to them, and they began to live by it, to fully live for the first time, not forsaking faith but finding faith in their generosity, in their caring.

Then came Juney to a band of humans, industrious, speaking with the words that she had taught humans to speak, building mud huts, using fire to keep warm and to cook their food, busy, ever busy. They were happy to see Juney, they petted her, they gathered around, then they were off, working, always working, improving, and improving, yes with love, but not so much love. Yes with caring, but not so much caring. In their work, their constant work, they had no time to come close to one another, always busy, always to the next task, cleaning, building. And Juney barked and ran from one to another, from the big man to the little woman to the great mother who was fat and jolly and working as hard as the rest to the children who were working to build huts, and she gathered them all. And she barked, slowly, then at last in her final message to them she gave the Bark of DOG:

> Take time to stop and smell the noses.

And they were abashed, they looked down. Then they turned to one another, they hugged one another, and they vowed never to forget that above all, the closeness and caring was most important.

Then Juney rested. And many young dogs came to her, the puppies of Sultan— Sultan, so young had he been when NAV ascended, now had puppies who were young and mature. And the puppies of the puppies of Sultan, and others, the followers and puppies of Paw, and of Ralph, and of Lady, and of Princess. Came they to her, for the disciples of NAV who were still able knew that Juney was old and that their puppies and the humans who followed them who could travel, who had the will through the power of love, would have only a little time to learn from Juney. And Juney taught them, there near the Ganges.

Now, in the 413th year after the Ascension of NAV, Juney was weak and weary. For many dog-years she had with great joy taken the way of NAV as an offering to all, to dogs, to the creatures of the forest and the mountains, and to humans. She asked for nothing but the chance to love, to care. The wisdom that NAV had taught her she gave to all who would listen. She had cared, she had licked even those who turned aside, she had brought hope to humans.

Then the puppies of Sultan were afraid, for Juney looked at one of them and said, "Prometheus, you have returned." And they sent for Sultan, for they knew not what they should do. And Juney turned to a young female, all brown and black, who had come from the Hindu Kush, and she said, "Ahh, Birta, you have come, too. I am glad to see you. Come let me smell you." And the young female was afraid. Then came Sultan from the Cedars of Lebanon, still strong in his love and in his body, strong in his mind, came he to Juney. And he saw that she was confused, and he barked to her, "Juney, do you not know? Prometheus is dead, you visited the tree that grows from his bones, you scattered the twelve cats of CAT there." And Juney nodded, yes, she knew, she had been confused. And Sultan said to her, "Do you not know? Birta is dead, you visited the place of her final breath and led the humans to mark it with a great stone." And Juney nodded, yes, she knew, she had been confused.

Then Juney knew that she must stop barking in the name of NAV and through Him of DOG lest she confuse others.

So she howled, a great howl, and came then from the Himalayas, came then Ursula, the great bear, the brown giantess. She came running, loping, until close to the Ganges came she near to Juney, she came snuffling, ambling with concern and with the love that Juney had taught her. Yes, with the love and caring that Juney had given her, that had made her life the life of more than a wild creature into a bear who loved, who taught the wild men of the great mountains, the hairy ones, so high in the Himalayas, Ursula took to them, too, the love of Dog.

And Juney told Ursula, "Arf, grrrr, hrrumph, hrrumph" mixing her talk with the talk of the bears, told she to Ursula that Juney's days must end before her teaching became confused. And of Ursula, Juney asked—not commanded— a favor: to end her life. For now, suddenly Juney could see, could see that in her death she could join in the great process of all, unseparated into a single being but part of the process of all, of NAV and DOG and all those who had gone before, not going to them but part of them as they would be part of her. In the light, then, and the flow of all would she be, if Ursula would help her.

Ursula, tears, uncomprehending, said "Hrrumph, hrrumph" meaning "Don't go, my teacher, my love." But Juney, with the little strength of mind she had left, focussed on Ursula, gazing at her with love, Juney's deep brown eyes focussed, and Ursula looked away, tears in her eyes, and turned suddenly and caught Juney in her arms, caught her as Ursula stood, towering over all those who were there. Paws behind Juney, her arms embracing her in a loving caress, Ursula licked Juney softly on her nose, and Juney looked into her eyes, and Ursula squeezed hard, harder, harder, and Juney sighed, and her last breath left her.

Ursula laid Juney down, and chipmunks, raccoons, birds, deer, all came, and the humans and the dogs that followed in the way of DOG through NAV stood back to let all the creatures come to Juney and smell of her for the last time. And lo, Juney smelled not of death, not of the last, but of the sweet smell that she had carried through life, the smell that all knew was the smell of the DOGGY LAMA.

Then Ursula, tears washing her face, dug into the ground, dug deeper and deeper. The others, the birds and creatures of the forest and desert, the humans, the dogs and puppies watched alert, but Ursula would not let them near. Not until she picked up Juney and placed her into the ground, into the deep, deep hole. Then the chipmunks and raccoons all helped to cover her with earth, to mound the moist black earth over her final resting spot. And came then Feral, knowing only now, nodding, wary, cautious, looking behind him, careful, came he to the mound of earth, and he planted there a dogwood tree above her grave.

Thus came Juney to her final days. And the days of many of the twelve disciples, too.

And we, now as always, remember the great gift of Santa Ursula, the gift she gave that hurt more than any giving could hurt, yet was welcome and which freed Juney. And we reckon it a great sign of love and faith to walk with a bear behind.

The Discovery of Boris, the Second DOGGY LAMA

Gathered after Juney was in the earth, when Ursula had groaned a last time, they began to dance. All yipped and played, even Feral, always alert and suspicious, frolicked with the rest, for death, they knew was no ending. They barked the words of NAV repeated so often by Juney:

> There is no end but only a continual beginning.

And they were happy. Gathered then were Bidú, and Feral, and Sultan, and coming slowly, so late, was Paw, old, still grumpy, but strong in the spirit of DOG, happy to let the puppies and the puppies of the puppies gambol around him, nipping at his side and even his neck. His black, black coat now with much grey, bald at his elbows and on his muzzle, he was glad, for he knew this was another beginning, licking the puppies, nuzzling up against the humans.

Came also Princess, the lovely one, shaggy and black and horrible to look at until you saw her eyes and the love that flowed from them, her rat-like tail wagging her greeting as she came from the foothills of the Hindu Kush. Not so strong but still so caring, she looked on the puppies and gathered them round with the human children, wagging her tail, licking and smelling them all, keeping them together while the others hunted and built a fire to cook the meat slowly.

But Lady, regal, white and golden her hair flowing out, her tail straight out, she had gone before, she had passed so many dog-years ago. All remembered her and thought of her in this time of great joy, of the joy of the passing of Juney to the flow and spirit of DOG.

And Ralph, with his purple coat, his look aslant and always joking, always wry and teaching through his jabs, through the laughter, he too had passed. His puppies and the humans that had followed him, some came with greetings from the Aral Sea, with hope in the love of those who were here, bringing with them his joking, his wry humor that bit with serious love and thought.

Spot, all white with a black spot on his brow, short hair, always jumping, ready always to spring against CAT, who sends her twelve cats and FERRATSI the great mountain lion, Spot, with the great heart, he could not come. Spot, of the great heart, the terror of the twelve cats of CAT had passed, had gone but had sent at the last a puppy of a puppy of Sultan, who was Spot's puppy, with greetings, greetings to all that they would someday be together again in the flow and spirit of DOG. And the little puppy, so small it was a wonder to all that she had been able to come so far from the Cedars of Lebanon, told how Spot had reminded them all that when Juney should be no more they must find the new DOGGY LAMA.

But Fido, the faithful one, small, with curling tail, black and white and tan and red, all intense, from near on the Euphrates to where NAV had preached so long, Fido, he did not come. He sent one of his acolytes, a big hairy dog that lumbered to them, telling of how Fido must stay there, near where NAV had preached and taught him, never forsaking NAV. And those of the twelve disciples of NAV who were there, being Paw, Bidú, Princess, Feral, and Sultan, they were puzzled, they could not understand how Fido conceived of the place of NAV that was not the place in his own heart. But they rejoiced to know that Fido was well and was teaching love through his example.

Then eating of the fat and the meat, of the dripping fat over the fire, sharing all, each more concerned that the other should eat and be satisfied, they lay at the fire, the dogs all snuffling and talking in their low, rumbling way, the puppies listening carefully, the humans adding what they remembered of Juney, and of Lady, and of Ralph, and of Spot, they talked and they shared the meat and the love of those who had passed and of those who were here. They knew that they never all would meet again, so many old, some so young, but they would share and remember this night. They were not chosen to be here but were only blessed to have the chance to share this moment of joy when Juney had become part of the flow of all. And as they talked they felt the responsibility, the great calling, to find the new DOGGY LAMA. They must go out, they must smell all, until they should find the one who would carry the message of DOG that NAV had begun and which Juney had shown.

The next day they set out, each to the place of home, the dogs searching for the next DOGGY LAMA, the dogs went out, for no human could find the smell of the holy one who would carry the teachings. They went. Some went to the North, the steppes of Bidú, following closely Bidú until he barked that they should go separate ways to look more widely. Some went to the South, past the Nile to where they found the first humans, and though those humans smelled not of the sanctity of DOG, they stayed there to teach them of the love of DOG. Some went to the East, to the land of the people who eat rice and raw fish and seaweed, looking always, smelling each human, each dog to see if they could find the new DOGGY LAMA, never forgetting to show those they met of the love of DOG, of the caring and the faithfulness of all. Some, too, went to the West, past the land of the Aral Sea, where Ralph had shown so many the love that surpasses understanding, where Ralph through jokes and his sarcasm had shown that love need not be always solemn but laughter and forgetting sorrows, too.

Until, nearly fourteen dog-years later, did the small puppy of a puppy of Sultan, who was the puppy of Spot, who had been one of the first to follow NAV, came to the farthest North, to a land all cold and barren. She found there humans, with tents made of reindeer skin, huddled near fires in the deep snow, and with them the great dogs that hunt wolves, so strong at the shoulders, with fur so heavy she could not believe it was possible. And among them she searched. She smelled all, first the humans, then the dogs. But she found not one who had the sweet smell, the smell she remembered from the death of Juney, the sweet smell greater than the smell of death.

Came then to the fires from guarding far and around, came then to the fires from hunting for all, came Boris, tall, white hair flowing, loping, strong, came he trotting to the fire to be sure that all were well. Boris, the wolf-hunting dog who had heard so long ago of NAV and had traveled to the Euphrates, to the heat that he could barely stand, traveling only at night. But he had found that NAV was no longer. He barked with those who were there, but he wanted more, he knew that he was only beginning to learn the love of DOG. So he set out to find Juney, the DOGGY LAMA, and he found her in her wanderings, he found her when she was crossing the mountains between the deserts East of the Euphrates and the fertile land of the Ganges. He learned from her, of the great love of DOG who enjoined us all to care, to lick those who would attack us, to lead to love by example and never force, to stop and smell the noses and be always generous. And he was happy and returned to the North, to his home, to the land of the flat-nosed humans and the wolf-hunting dogs. He returned and was more thoughtful of all, more caring of the children and puppies, barking strongly to keep away the snow leopards, those followers of CAT, for Juney had warned him of CAT and of FERRATSI the mountain lion who would turn all from the love of DOG to the fear and hatred that CAT would demand. And Boris barked to let the twelve cats of CAT know that he was here, that no one would harm the body or spirit of those at this camp so long as he could stand.

Yet Boris was uneasy. He could not understand the flow of all, how we become one when we pass beyond the world of bodies. He meditated. In the position of meditation, lying with his paws stretched in front, his head raised looking straight ahead, his focus on the distance, his breathing regular, he meditated, yet alert, always alert for the danger of the followers of CAT. He meditated, but never for long, for he was to protect those he loved, to remind them of love through his example of unconditional faithfulness, to provide for them in the hunt. He meditated on DOG, on how to achieve the Doghead so as to be free of fear and ever more open to love.

And through his meditation he began to see. He heard the bark of NAV, he heard the bark of Juney, knowing not that she had passed, he heard, first faintly then so strong the Bark of DOG. And he came to know that we are not separate. We are no more separate and individual than the water of the Black Sea is separate and distinct from the other waters that cover the earth, that we are no more separate than the wind that blows across our face is separate from all the air that covers the earth. We are all one in the flow of life, only separate in the perception of DOG, but our separateness, he finally saw, is an illusion. Our separateness is only a way of seeing ourselves and others, of seeing the tree as distinct from us, of seeing the deer we are ready to eat as not one with us, of thinking that NAV and Juney were separate when they are all with us in the flow of all. Then freed from the illusion of individuality, freed from the illusion that keeps us separate from others, freed from the illusion that keeps us from truly loving, he was free. And he began to teach. He barked slowly, very slowly, returning again and again to meditate, to secure the knowledge that he could pass on to all so that all could see that love is joy, that death is no cause for sorrow, that the sufferings we feel are the illusion of our separateness. He taught, but always alert. Until that small puppy of a puppy of Sultan, who was the puppy of Spot, who had been one of the first to follow NAV, came to the farthest North and saw Boris approaching the fire. The puppy, she was tired, lame from her wandering, cold, too, in the North, yet she rose from the fire and went to Boris and smelled him. And she knew the smell, the sweet smell that is greater than the smell of death. She knew the smell, and she howled. All looked at her, the dogs alert, the humans worried, concerned for her, and she howled again, greatly. Then she yipped, she jumped, she nipped at the neck of each dog, she threw herself joyfully on the chest of each human, she herded the children and puppies all in front of Boris. And she barked:

Here is he, the DOGGY LAMA, the teacher and great spirit of us all.

And those who knew of Juney who had been the DOGGY LAMA were amazed. But they came to Boris who now had the sweet smell that is greater than the smell of death, so strong was the smell that even the humans could recognize it.

And they bowed down. And Boris, bewildered, would not let them bow, for he, too bowed down, thinking only of DOG and the teachings of NAV, and the bows became play-bows, and the barking became bow wows, and they all danced, circling the fire, with Boris following, then leading, then following, joyfully with them, not realizing that he was truly the DOGGY LAMA. But the small puppy of a puppy of Sultan, who was the puppy of Spot, who had been one of the first to follow NAV, she told him, and all around told him of his new smell, of the odor of sanctity that he carried. So he bowed before them, he bowed and begged their help, he begged for the help and caring that would let him teach. And each dog went to him and licked his muzzle, and he licked theirs. And each human went to him and petted him, stroking his strong shoulder and head, and was licked by him.

Boris then felt that he should go, that he should set out from his home to take the Bark of DOG to all, as Juney the first DOGGY LAMA had done. But those around him were fearful. How could they survive without his care? And he knew that he must teach more there, to those who would come to him as he taught the pack of dogs and humans who still must learn of the unconditional love of DOG that knows not guilt nor fear nor pride.

Then the small puppy of a puppy of Sultan, who was Spot's puppy, she shook herself, shaking off the snow, uncurling her legs, stretching with tail in the air and paws so far in front, stretching, ready now to leave, to tell all that there is a DOGGY LAMA again, new and with wisdom to share. She sniffed the air, she went to Boris and licked him, she pressed against his side, smelled him once more. And as she turned, trotting away she heard Boris give the greeting of the North, the greeting of those in the faith of dog, "Dogsvadanya."

The Pilgrimage of Tiny

Boris, now the Second DOGGY LAMA, stayed in the white snow that covered his home in the North. He stopped at a gathering of people and dogs. Cold it was, but not bitter, and for Boris of the North it was a delight to be there with the husky dogs of the heavy grey fur who had heard of DOG and of NAV, but not yet of Juney, and with the humans who were ready, who were open to love having learned from the husky dogs, the husky dogs who were willing to pull sleds for them, showing them their loyalty and faith and love. He stopped there to teach, to meditate, too, when all were asleep, and to learn. Always the DOGGY LAMA must learn, for love is a never-ending joy with many manifestations.

There, in the cold, he saw coming in the swirl of snow a tiny creature, so tiny he could not imagine that it was a dog until he caught the scent. Yes, a dog so small, with big ears, almost hairless, who had traveled so far to learn. He had left his home in the desert near the great lake in the middle of Aztechoia, in a land so far away that Boris strained to imagine. So far, from a hot desert, in a continent that was not of the lands that Boris and the twelve disciples of NAV had known. He, Tiny, the smallest of the small dogs had heard the call of NAV from the birds that had come to his land when he was only a puppy. All the others had ignored it, a strange call of love in the twitter, a call of peace that other dogs thought only silly, a rumor from afar. But Tiny had listened. He had dreamed a dream of peace. He told his sister Rosabella, who could not believe. He told her of a dog called NAV, a dog who was the only puppy of DOG, who could heal suffering through his bark of love, not healing wounds, not healing disease, but healing the sickness unto death of despair. Rosabella loved Tiny's barking, his stories that he heard from the birds, but she could not believe.
And yet, yet when he barked that he must go, he must find NAV to learn, she followed, charmed and hopeful in his dream, but not believing. So they walked North, across a great desert, so hot they could walk only at night. Rosabella was afraid, for there were mountain lions, there were rattlesnakes, there were cacti with spines so sharp they could pierce a paw, and there was no food, no water. But DOG provided, for He saw that Tiny and Rosabella were on a great journey, a journey that would lead them to Him, a journey they must make to learn of love. So each morning when they were ready to stop traveling they found a clear pool of water, very small and clear, that seemed a mirage until they approached it and drank. And they found at each pool two mice, left there by the ravens that seemed so savage, crying and circling, but were told by Him who smells all to feed these pilgrims.

They came then to a river, the Grand River of the North. They waited for the hot, hot summer, the summer when at last the Grand River of the North was only a trickle, when even Tiny and Rosabella could pick their way across, tiny feet, walking, wading, swimming. They continued to the North, and then Rosabella feared more, for there was cold. They could not continue, they could not, for they had no fur, no way to warm themselves. And DOG led them to a cave, there in the great mountains of the North, where slept a bear. And they crept up to the bear, and they lay beside him in his sleep, lay beside him in his warmth, and the bear would not awaken, until it would be warm enough for them to leave the cave and begin their journey again.

Thus passed six dog-years travelling, and still Tiny knew they had far to go, for the birds had told him to follow the North Star until they were to go left at the great river that flows to the sea. In the Spring of the seventh dog-year they came to a wide, fast-flowing stream, so fast, so wide, yet Tiny knew they had to cross. They lay there, footsore, weary. Tiny cajoled Rosabella to be brave and hopeful, though they could see no way to cross the river. And then came to them a bear, for all bears had now heard of Ursula, the bear who had sacrificed by giving the great gift of passing to Juney, one came to them, growling and hrrumphing, and Rosabella was greatly afraid. But Tiny could see that the bear, Ursus Minor, black and grizzly, was there to help them, that DOG had sent him, and Tiny climbed upon the back of Ursus Minor and barked for Rosabella to come up to him. And together they rode upon the broad back of Ursus Minor while he swam across the great river. As he came to the other side Ursus Minor forgot and shook himself greatly, he shook and shook to rid himself of water, and Tiny and Rosabella flew off, almost as high as the birds. Rosabella barked in great fear, certain they would now fall and be crushed upon the rocks. Then two great ravens, cawing, flew close, one grasping Rosabella in his talons, one grasping Tiny in her talons, and they flew up. Then Rosabella yipped and howled a most horrible howl. But Tiny was thrilled, he knew this was the paw of DOG, come to save them for His mission, and he barked, "Arf, we go into the wild blue yonder, flying high into the sky." And the two ravens, black as the burnt flesh of untended meat over a fire, the ravens flew down with Rosabella and Tiny and placed them softly on the ground.

So Tiny and Rosabella followed the river to the sea and continued North along the coast of the sea, along the ocean, past warm waters and then colder waters, past a glacier where they had to pick their way among rocks and ice, along the shore, provided each night with two mice from the goodness of the ravens who soared, of the ravens who saw that no bird would molest them. Came they then to a narrow land, with water on each side, so narrow, a bridge from the great land they were on to another great land, at the sea of the great white bears, the Bearing Sea. They crossed the narrow land when it was near to the autumn, when the air was cold at night, though the days were warm, when the flowers were shriveled, when the mice were burrowing into the ground with their seeds ready for the long, long night of winter. They continued, but now there was no bear, no cave, only the long, flat tundra ahead. And Rosabella howled, for though she wanted the peace that Tiny told her of, though she wanted to learn to be loving and caring, she had no faith, no certainty. Then DOG entered her heart, He barked to her, and she knew, she knew that she would continue in His care, until Tiny would come to one who would teach, but she would not learn, she would not be there. The love she had, the love she would give is the love for Tiny her brother, the love of protecting him.

And they continued in the cold, their paws frozen at night and unfrozen at day, digging into the snow for warmth, until the night when they heard the awful screech of a cat, of a mountain lion, of FERRATSI, who had discovered their journey, who wanted none to learn of the love of DOG. And Tiny was sore afraid. But Rosabella was not. She jumped up, she growled in her high screeching yip, matching screech for screech, ready to attack, fierce beyond any measure for one so small. And came then the smell of cat, the stink and reek of cat—it was FEAR and VENGEANCE, two cats of CAT, who stalked close. They attacked, and Tiny was held down by FEAR, until Rosabella attacked, she ripped at FEAR, she nipped VENGEANCE on her teats, she bit FEAR and bit him again, but she was weak without the power of faith in DOG. She fought, and then Tiny became great, he shook off FEAR, he barked with a bark of a great dog, of a dog that was huge, filled as he was with the knowledge that DOG is love. And FEAR and VENGEANCE slunk off. But as they went, VENGEANCE with a great swipe of her paw slashed Rosabella across the muzzle, clawing across the face of Rosabella, and Rosabella could see no more. Rosabella, the sister of Tiny, could not see, nor could she walk, for FEAR had bit her paw, the left front paw, that dangled from a tendon. She could not walk, then she could not see; but she would not whine. She came close to Tiny, hobbling on three legs, she came to him, and she panted in her weak breath, "Do not stop for me, go my brother, my love, go to learn of love and take the message of DOG to our brothers and sisters at home in the desert and cactus, the land of sweet morning air after the rain, go to learn and to return. I shall never meet the teacher of the ways of DOG, but you shall, and you shall have the great care to return to our land to teach, the land I shall never see again." And she passed. And the ravens above circled, they called, and a great tear from a raven dropped on what was once the body of Rosabella, and another raven flew by and a great tear dropped, and another tear, and another tear, and another, and the tears covered Rosabella, covered her and froze, and Rosabella was cased with ice, clear, crystal ice. Then Tiny dug into the frozen ground, he dug with his small, small paws, he dug for one day and one night, not thinking of cold or hunger, until he had a place in the earth for Rosabella, in the earth that never thaws, and there he placed her body, beautiful beyond imagining, her sufferings for all to see, he placed her there in her shield of crystal ice, and he covered her, scratching the dirt back to cover her crystal sepulchre, and he marked the place with his water. And there, in the frozen tundra, in the cold of winter, a cactus and a second cactus grew, all prickly as the cacti of the land where Rosabella had longed to be, of the land of warmth and sun, now grew a prickly pair, and upon each a small yellow flower bloomed, the flower of Rosabella. Rosabella, who died that Tiny might live to learn of DOG, Rosabella the protector of kin, though she never learned the love of DOG, she had love enough to sacrifice herself for her brother and for the hope of DOG.

So Tiny mourned for seven days and seven nights, nourished by the mice left by the ravens. He mourned, for he knew not yet that love is greater than death, he knew not that Rosabella had not gone but continued in the great flow of all. He would learn, he would learn that through suffering, through sacrifice does love grow stronger, the love that DOG lets us learn, the love that is stronger than hate and fear and pride. He would learn. After seven days and seven nights he had mourned enough, the ravens cawed. So he continued west, crossing the wide, flat tundra, and in only two days he saw the fires of the camp of Boris, the Second DOGGY LAMA.

We pray to you now and ever for our kin and the dreams they have, Santa Rosabella.

She Who Loves the Lowest

She, the small puppy of a puppy of Sultan, who was the puppy of Spot, who had been one of the first to follow NAV, was called by some the Discoverer, for it was she who had discovered Boris, the Second DOGGY LAMA. And by others she was called She Who Whiffs the Sweet Smell, for it was she who first sniffed the sweet smell of the DOGGY LAMA emanating from Boris.

When she left Boris, she traveled to the steppes. There she told Bidú, who rejoiced to hear of the new DOGGY LAMA. Old as he was, with his hips sore and out of joint, he would not travel. But he sent one of his puppies to learn from Boris. And he sent others to tell of the revealing of the Second DOGGY LAMA.

Traveled she then to the fertile ground near the Ganges, where she found Paw, so old, yet strong and preaching still, smoking his cigars, she told him and his followers of Boris the DOGGY LAMA. And Paw saw many of his puppies and their puppies and their puppies jump and frolic and disperse to tell all of the revealing of Boris.

She traveled then to the woods near the Aral Sea, to the land where Ralph had taught and shown of love, and there the Ralphists welcomed her, laughing at her stories, rejoicing in the knowledge that a new DOGGY LAMA would bring more wisdom, more help for them to follow in the path of love that NAV first taught and that Juney had widened. And laughing, prodding and joking, play-bowing and bow wowing, they chose three of themselves, two humans and one dog, to venture out and tell all of the DOGGY LAMA who would keep them strong in the faith of DOG.

Finally she came to the cedars of Lebanon, to the land of Spot, her great grandfather who had passed so long ago, and the land of Sultan, her grandfather, and she barked with joy to be with those who loved as well as she, who could give. Sultan wagged his tail, he wagged and wagged so much to see his beloved granddaughter that his whole body shook. They jumped, they licked, they smelled, they howled and yipped, and all were joyous. And they brought the message to the humans they were teaching, to the humans who had learned to trust by trusting the dogs that Sultan had told of the love of DOG. All were glad that the DOGGY LAMA, though far from them, would teach and lead them to more wisdom, though it might be many years before they would hear his message.

From these places other dogs went out, and with them humans, to tell all of the great joy of a new DOGGY LAMA, of Boris, who taught of the flow of all, the flow of all that Juney had known only at the moment when she was about to die. Boris had found it, found it from what he had learned from her and from his meditation, and would give to all the knowledge that there is no end, no beginning, but only the flow, the becoming that is always becoming.

But she, the Discover, She Who Whiffs the Sweet Smell, would not stop with those she loved, there among the cedars of Lebanon. There were many in that place who knew of DOG, who could help those who were helpless, who could teach of love. No, she must travel to find where she could help. She barked goodbye to the memory of Spot, goodbye to Sultan, goodbye to her mother and father, goodbye to the other puppies she had suckled with, goodbye to their puppies, she barked goodbye. This was her great sacrifice, to leave those whom she loved to travel to give love to those whom she knew not.

She traveled South, near to the Dead Sea, near to Kelev Tov from whence Juney had come so long ago. She traveled farther South, farther, until she reached a small place of a few huts near caves that were shelters, too. There she found humans and a few dogs. But the dogs were filled with fear, and the humans were not kind. She went to the dogs, she taught them to love, to trust, to go beyond fear to let the humans touch them, to go beyond the first kick or stone and to return, again and again, crouching low, whining, until the humans would touch them, would stroke them, would let them come into their hearts. And the humans were proud, believing they had tamed the wild dogs, and each man pointed to his dog, each woman to her dog, as if it were a possession, comparing, each proclaiming the virtues of their dog. They were proud, each felt the love of the dog that had picked them as if the man had picked it, as if the woman were the master, proud in the love of their dogs. And the Discoverer, She Who Whiffs the Sweet Smell, was sad, for this was not the love of DOG that dogs could teach. This was only the love of getting, of being loved.

And she saw among the humans one who was twisted, with black hair unkempt dragging around his face, with eyes that were not clear, who talked and talked and talked to himself, of gods and demons and fear and the night. He walked in circles and he was distressed but he did not know of his distress. He saw illusions that filled him with fear. He had killed when the men had fought other people, he had killed and seen his fellows kill. Even those who could not stand they killed, clubbing them as they lay, as they begged for mercy, even the babies they had cut apart, bloody, so bloody, so bloody. So that they could be free. And he could not stop thinking of the killing, of the love that he had killed.

He was shunned by all, he was like unto a leper, with no sores but the sores of his mind, his disease of his madness they shunned lest they be infected with the pus of his dreams.

And she, the Discoverer, She Who Whiffs the Sweet Smell, she had compassion for him, not only for his distress but because she could smell in his life the deep love that had driven him into guilt and fear. She could see in his movements, in the jerk and catch of his walk, in his disconnected speech, she could see the broken bits of love that tormented him, for he could not find how to put them back together in the fear and guilt and regret of all that he had done when he had killed. And she, the Discoverer, She Who Whiffs the Sweet Smell, she went up to him and lay by his side. He noticed her not, but walked in a circle, and in a circle again, and she crept closer, she touched his leg. He drew back, as if he—not she—were unclean. Yet she licked him. And he said, "Touch me not, for I am not clean." Yet she licked him again, recognizing in him the great love that had soured yet could still be fresh. And she looked into his eyes. And for the first time in many, many years his eyes saw. He looked into her eyes, and he found there love, love that he had not killed, love that was offered with no asking. And he stopped. Then he continued, the break in his illusions only a small break, and he walked in circles, and he talked. But he stopped, and he petted her. And she licked him and nuzzled close to him. And for a moment, for only a moment, he felt a small joy. But he remembered the horror he had seen, the horror he had done, and he walked another circle.

The next day the Discoverer, She Who Whiffs the Sweet Smell, would not leave his side, not to eat nor to drink. He knew still to eat and drink, though little there was, only the scraps that the other humans would not touch but which the dogs in their compassion would not eat and left for him. He went, and she went with him, he ate and he looked, quizzically, as if remembering some other life, and he offered to her a small bone, and then a bigger bone, and then he pushed all that there was to her, and hurried away. But she would not eat, she would go with him, and she whined and brought him back to the bones and little meat, and they ate together.

Another day, and another day, and another day, and the Discoverer, She Who Whiffs the Sweet Smell, the most magnificent of all the dogs any human had ever seen, she who was tall, and swift, beautiful in shape and alertness, the most beautiful of silky coats, she would not leave the side of him who suffered. And the humans could not understand. He was mad, he was the crazy one, he did not deserve such a magnificent dog. He deserved no love at all. Each tried to entice her away from the distressed one, offering her the best meat, shunning their own dogs, but she would not leave the side of the distressed one. And the humans saw in her the unconditional love they had not known, the love that finds in its beloved all of the world, and they saw that there was something, some deep source in the mad one that she, the Discoverer, She Who Whiffs the Sweet Smell, had found. They saw that each is worthy of love, even the lowest among us. And they became ashamed. And each grieved greatly for the pride they had shown, for the evil they had done, and they retreated, each away from the others. Yet with each man went his dog, with each woman her dog. And they learned, the dogs and the humans, to love. And the next morning, each came out from his cave, each from her hut, and looked at one another, abashed, yet sweetly for they had learned in the long night, each at the side of a dog that loved and asked for nothing, they had learned of love that gives and does not take, of love that fears killing a human or dog more than it fears death. And they gathered around and made a sweet fire in the cold early morning, seeing the sun coming up over the mountains in the East, rosy-fingered dawn spreading over the desert, and they all knew that life had only then begun. That freedom was not won with killing but with love.

And she, the Discoverer, She Who Whiffs the Sweet Smell, stayed all her life with the one who was distressed, the one who would walk in circles, for she knew that his love was finding out its way in his jerking and talking. And he became calmer, though not clear, he stroked her, he petted her, he learned to love again, though never clearly. And the humans offered to them the first meat of the slaughter of any sheep, the cooked heart and the dripping fat. And they saw in his madness the sign of love, they saw in his madness the horror of killing, and they learned.

And she, the Discoverer, She Who Whiffs the Sweet Smell, became known as She Who Loves the Lowest. This is good, she thought. "Discoverer," "She Who Whiffs the Sweet Smell," those were titles that were not her. Any dog who had been looking, who had known the sweet smell, would have discovered Boris and his power of love to be the Second DOGGY LAMA. It was her luck, not anything special of her, that had found Boris in his revealing. What was special about her was her deep love for the distressed one, the love she gave and gave and gave, and she was happy to be known as She Who Loves the Lowest. And she told each dog that what was special about each of us is our love, our special love for the one to whom we wish to give our love, and then think no more of wishing but only of loving, of the attachment that cannot die. This is what is special, this she taught to them all, both human and dog, by example, by her unconditional love and her teaching. She let them know what she had learned so long ago from the teachers of those who had learned from NAV:

There is no way to peace, peace is the way.

And she remained with the distressed one, comforting and helping, all her life. And she knew that this was a good life, a life no better could be hoped for, for she loved and she taught others to love, and in the love they found some peace.

The Great Schism

Then to Fido came the bark that Juney had died, had passed, had passed into what she barked at the end was the great flow of all. And then came the bark that a new DOGGY LAMA had been discovered, that a puppy of a puppy of Sultan, who was the puppy of Spot, who had been one of the first to follow NAV, had smelled the sweet smell that is greater than the smell of death, and now Boris was proclaimed the Second DOGGY LAMA. Boris, a dog of the North, of the kind that hunt wolves, with white flowing hair, who had studied with Juney and who had meditated, Boris is now the DOGGY LAMA.

And Fido howled, he howled with a cry so longing, so mournful, so lonely, so full of death, that all on the Euphrates could hear and were filled with fear and compassion. Fido howled. And Fido howled. He could not abide—no, no, another teacher in the line of NAV, and he, Fido, was farther now from NAV. He, Fido, who had been so close to NAV in the life of NAV, he, Fido, who could remember each bark of NAV, each wag of his tail, each lick of his tongue, farther still from NAV by the intercession of another, a stranger, one not even known to NAV, now the DOGGY LAMA. Fido howled. It was wrong, wrong—for he was closest to NAV, he felt the loss of NAV each day, each night. He was closest, he knew best how to teach, he Fido, for he was the puppy of NAV, the Hidden One. Proclaimed only now, he barked. Yes, Fido, the puppy of NAV, who would teach the great barks of NAV.

And as he barked his heritage for all to hear, two humans came to his camp. They called in a strange and screeching voice that Fido was right, that Fido was the puppy of NAV, that they would follow only him, not the imposter, the interceder Boris. They came covered in skins only half-tanned—to cover the smell of cat. For these were FEAR and PRIDE, two of the twelve cats of CAT sent by FERRATSI the mountain lion. FEAR, strong in her ability to persuade humans to accept her and PRIDE and all the other cats of CAT. And PRIDE, her constant companion, he who was small but made himself look big, who strutted but in a weak catwalk, whispered to Fido that yes, he is the puppy of NAV, yes, he is the great teacher, yes he will lead all to the teachings of NAV, for he is great, he is powerful in his shared blood of NAV. And Fido, crazed with the loss of NAV, crazed with FEAR and PRIDE, believed his own telling, that he was the puppy of NAV and he would lead all.

Fido could not see that these strange humans were FEAR and PRIDE disguised as friends, he could not smell their cattiness. FERRATSI, prowling, always prowling in the desert, far from the camp, could hear the howling and the screeching, and she was happy, she mewed with contentment, for the power of DOG was soon to be broken, the followers of DOG soon to be scattered into many camps, each led by one of the cats of CAT, all directed by FEAR and PRIDE. Thus was the beginning of the Great Schism.

The many followers of DOG along the Euphrates heard the bark of Fido. And some believed because they wanted to believe that they, too, were close to NAV through Fido, as if NAV were still alive in His puppy. The humans cried and danced that the Hidden One was revealed. And many dogs, especially the young, came to follow Fido. Fido believed he was the puppy of NAV because FEAR and PRIDE kept close to him, encouraging him, telling him in soft almost mewing voices that he was great, Fido the son of NAV, who was the only puppy of DOG.

Then FEAR and PRIDE hinted and hinted until Fido barked that all who follow DOG should follow him, Fido, the son of NAV. And they would be called Sonny's dogs and people. And henceforth they were called Sonnys.

Then PRIDE insinuated herself more into Fido's will, and Fido declared that a great palace should be built at the side of the Euphrates, a palace that all could see was the palace of the son of NAV, the great teacher. And over the high door of the palace the humans carved an image of Fido, who was now known as the SON of the SON of DOG.

The humans continued in obeisance to Fido, while all the time the closest to him were FEAR and PRIDE, insinuated, always there, helping Fido with his teaching, guiding away from the love of DOG and into the world of CAT. Now HATE, a twisted, snarling cat, came from the desert at the command of FERRATSI, came looking like a crippled man, covered also in half-tanned skins to cover his catty smell, limping, calling in a mewing voice that he, too, would join the followers of Fido. And FEAR and PRIDE knew their brother, and they were glad, for with his help they would surely break the power of DOG upon the earth. They whispered, they purred to Fido that here was a crippled one, one who deserved compassion, yet wise, that he would teach with them. And Fido, governed always by FEAR and PRIDE, welcomed HATE into his camp.

Then HATE purred into the ear of Fido. And Fido declared that all who did not follow him were not true followers of DOG. That all who did not follow him were outcast, heretics, and must be exiled. Those who did not follow Fido were first told to leave, then bitten to frighten them away, then, in a horrible frenzy on an overcast night, on a night of no moon, the followers of Fido attacked a camp of humans and dogs near the palace, humans and dogs who would not acknowledge Fido as their true leader. The Sonnys attacked them, and they killed three before the others fled. These, the three martyrs of the faith of DOG, helpless and unwilling to fight, for they knew that love does not fight, that it is better to die than to kill a human or dog, so they were torn apart, ripped, bloody, torn by the dogs and clubbed by the humans who were Sonnys. But FEAR and PRIDE and HATE did not attack; they watched, their yellow and green eyes surveying all, mewing in contentment. Their work had begun well.

Those who followed the way of DOG fled, those who knew that love is the way, not hate, not power, they went through the desert. They went over the mountains and barked and said to all how Fido now believed that he was the puppy of NAV, how some strange humans whispered always in his ear, how they were hounded from their homes, bitten and chased, and three were killed by the followers of Fido. They said it was the Great Schism.

The followers of DOG wandered, homeless. They called, and the words and the bark went far, went to the East, to the West, to the South, to the North, across green fields and the deserts, across the valleys and the mountains, across the rivers and the seas, the bark went out. And Boris, the Second DOGGY LAMA, heard in garbled news of the Great Schism. He could not believe that one who had been a disciple of NAV, who had been with NAV at the first, could break from the love of DOG. He could not believe that Fido, whose name and story he knew from Juney, could kill in the name of the love of DOG. But another dog came, and then a human who had been there in the attack upon the followers of DOG, chilled and shivering came they to tell all of the Great Schism: they had seen the humans and dogs kill in the name of love. And Boris believed.

Then Boris set out from the North to travel to the Euphrates. And he sent his young companions, fiery and happy young dogs that were close to him, to tell the last of the disciples of NAV of the horror that had fallen on the followers of DOG.

But Bidú, the great protector, Bidú with black and white fur flying wildly, giant that he was, with his square face, his huge head, powerful shoulders, who would help all those in need, Bidú could not come. He had breathed his last, clawing, fighting with VENGEANCE and GLUTTONY who had come to his camp, certain of their power and the waning of the power of DOG in the world. They had come with FERRATSI. Bidú was old, his followers bewildered by talk of a puppy of NAV now revealed, and VENGEANCE and GLUTTONY set on Bidú, and though many would help the great and once-powerful protector, they were frozen in fear, for VENGEANCE and GLUTTONY seemed suddenly so great. And Bidú barked greatly, deep barks from the depth of his chest, great barks, but VENGEANCE and GLUTTONY were not afraid, FERRATSI only mewed a laugh, as they set harder on Bidú, and though strong in the faith of DOG, he was weak in his body, being already 816 years old, and he could not fight to fight them hard. He snapped, he bit, he grabbed the fur of GLUTTONY, but no blood, only fur, and they scratched him, they clawed him, they bit until FERRATSI came and with a great blow of his paw hit Bidú who staggered, and VENGEANCE jumped upon his back and bit his neck, and Bidú fell, never to move again, his neck broken. Bidú, the great protector, lay dead, and many of the humans and dogs were awed and they cowered before these cats, and pledged their loyalty to those so powerful. Then VENGEANCE and GLUTTONY and FERRATSI had the humans and dogs build a great fire to celebrate the power of CAT. They made sacrifice of small birds and mice and ate the meat. Other dogs and humans, those who would not follow CAT, fled, afraid but sure of their love of each other, of Bidú. They fled. But some would not leave Bidú, now torn into many parts. They would not let him lie unburied, unmourned. And when VENGEANCE and GLUTTONY and FERRATSI were sated with meat from the sacrifice, when the humans and dogs who followed them cowered in their huts, these true followers of DOG slinked into the camp, they found the paw of Bidú, they found his powerful shoulders, they found his square gigantic head, they gathered all these of the great protector and teacher of the way of DOG, and they carried them, heavy as they were, they carried them for one day, and then another day, and the flesh did not smell of death but stayed fresh and sweet as Bidú had been fresh and sweet to all in his life. And on the third day they found a cave in a cliff, and they placed in the cave all that remained of Bidú. They covered his torn body with dirt, and they remembered him, all trembling yet filled with the joy and love of DOG that NAV had led them to. And they pushed a great rock across the face of the cave, a rock so none could enter, and Bidú rests there still.

No, Bidú could not come. But Sultan, the puppy of Spot, the second generation of those who would follow DOG through NAV, he who had taught so long, whose puppies now went across the deserts and mountains and seas to teach, Sultan came, not young but in his 634th year still able to stride, to walk with power. He asked none to come with him. But many came, the humans whom he had loved, the puppies he had given life to, so many of those who could, came walking with him. Yet some slinked back, they had heard the stories, they were afraid.

Came also Princess, the lovely one, shaggy and black and horrible to look at until you saw her eyes and the love that flowed from them, her rat-like tail wagging her greeting, came she from the foothills of the Hindu Kush. She came and joined Boris. Though weak she walked with the love of DOG in her heart. Her rat-like tail wagging, she encouraged all to follow, to lead.

Then came Paw, the gruff, the surly who hid his great heart behind his black, black short coat, big, from the fertile ground near the Ganges, a cigar in his mouth, drooling, sniffing. He who had with such power traveled so far in the past, who had preached the word of DOG through NAV, who had trotted almost sideways great distances, his great black coat now flecked with so much grey, he could only hobble, his hips almost out of joint, great pain, he would not be dissuaded by those who loved him most, he must come, his great companion Fido was in trouble, Fido whose love of NAV knew no bounds had now bounded beyond the love of NAV. Fido, Paw barked, needed him. And he would come. Such pain in his walk, but no pain to the pain in his heart that Fido, who had been so close to NAV, had strayed and was in the thrall of some horror that had broken him away from the love of DOG. Then came a great dog, a massive dog, taller by twice than Paw, a mastiff so black, this great powerful dog came up to Paw. His great jaws drooling, he came to Paw and lay down next to him. He whimpered, and whimpered again, and Paw saw that it was good, and he climbed upon the back of the great mastiff. And the mastiff, as with no weight at all, carried Paw to the meeting that all dreaded and hoped for, the chance they would have to bark with Fido.

And they joined, Paw, Sultan, Princess, and Boris, at the great mountains between the land of the fertile fields of the Ganges and the desert and oases of the land of the Euphrates. Boris sniffed each of them, for these were the disciples of NAV, the last of the generation that had known NAV, all here except for Fido. Then as they climbed to the highest pass that would lead to the desert and then to the fertile valley of the Euphrates, came Feral, the wild one, unkempt, with head too big and paws too small, came he from the wild places in India, absent so long they knew not that he lived, the last of the disciples of NAV. He came alone, looking to the left, to the right, behind, but not ahead. Careful, wary, he came alone and prowled around the camp they made that night. He came to Boris, he smelled Boris, and Feral barked a small bark and licked and was licked, he hurriedly smelled and was smelled by Paw, by Sultan, by Princess, then he ran to the edge of the camp, prowling, never resting, always alert.

They paused there at the pass in the high mountains, resting around a fire. Then came Princess to Boris and she barked, "You must lead us, you who are wise." Sultan, too, came to Boris and barked, "You must lead us, you who are wise." Came Paw, too, and barked, "You must lead us, you who are wise." For though they had been with NAV, though they were the last of the twelve disciples of NAV, they had not the wisdom they could smell upon Boris. And Feral, at the edge of the camp heard their barks, and he looked to the left, he looked to the right, he scurried around the camp and stopped only for a moment near the fire and barked a small bark that he would follow Boris. And Boris whimpered softly, "I cannot lead. I can only teach. I can only walk in the way of love that NAV, the only puppy of DOG, has taught us that I learned from the bark of Juney. I will go with you, for you are the ones who were close with NAV, who knew his smell, who heard his bark. Together we will go, each of us with our own wisdom, for there is no wisdom greater than love."

The next day they descended to the desert, the desert that would lead to the meeting they all dreaded and hoped for, the chance they would have to bark with Fido. In the desert, in the heat, Boris suffered, Boris of the Arctic North, Boris with his long white hair, thick upon his back, thick upon his chest, panting he continued, ever panting. The young ones trotted ahead quickly to find water, to bring water to Boris. He continued, never whimpering, slowly but with a sure step. Not following, not leading, Boris was only one among them, with Paw upon the back of the great mastiff, with Sultan near, with Princess softly, slowly padding with them. But Feral prowled at the edge, round and round, old but vigorous, alert, always alert.

They came close to the Euphrates and stopped there. The dogs huddled close, troubled in their dreams, the humans murmuring close with fear. And the next day they came to the Euphrates near to the palace of Fido. And they saw on the other shore, across the fast flowing waters, the muddy waters that separated them, the followers of Fido, massed, and Fido in the distance, on a great dias at the front of the palace, resting and looking out across the Euphrates, with FEAR and PRIDE and HATE at his side.

Then the humans with Paw and Princess and Sultan and Boris, they grew angry, they saw the palace with the carved image of Fido, and Fido surveying all. They grew angry, and those who had been at the camp of Fido when his followers set upon the humans and dogs, those who had seen the blood of their fellows soak into the sand, they cried out, "Vengeance," they cried, "Vengeance, destroy the false prophet." They held clubs in their hands, they cried of power. Then Boris padded before them. He howled a howl of misery. "Are we the true followers of DOG if we hate? Are we the true followers of DOG if we would destroy? Do you not know that it is better to die than to kill? To kill a human, to kill a dog is the way of CAT. There is no way to love except to love. VENGEANCE is a cat, one of the twelve cats of CAT who has entered your hearts. We must join with those across the river, we must join with them in love. And if they strike you, turn the other side of your muzzle. Let them strike, let us die, but do not let us kill, do not let us approach them with hate. That is the way of CAT. The way of DOG is love, is loyalty, is faith. Fido is one of us. He has strayed from the way of DOG, but he is one of us, as are all those who follow him, all those massed there across the river. We cannot join with them in hate but only in love."

And the humans were ashamed, they bowed their heads. And the young dogs who had barked for blood were ashamed, they bowed their heads, they put their tails between their legs, they whimpered. But they were afraid, for though they had love, they had not the faith that could sustain them to face death for a love so uncertain from those across the river.

Then slowly came Paw to the front. Paw, the gruff, the surly who hid his great heart behind his black and now grey short coat, big, from the fertile ground near the Ganges, a cigar in his mouth, drooling, sniffing, he limped slowly to the front, ignoring the great pain in his hips and shoulders, came he before the humans and dogs near the river. He stopped. He howled. Then slowly came Princess, the lovely one, shaggy and black and horrible to look at until you saw her eyes and the love that flowed from them, her rat-like tail wagging her greeting, she from the foothills of the Hindu Kush, she stepped forward, step by step to the front. She stopped. She howled. Then slowly came Sultan, the puppy of Spot, the second generation of those who would follow DOG through NAV, he walked surely and strongly to the front. He stopped. He howled. And then came Feral, the wild one, unkempt, with head too big and paws too small, from the wild places in India, he sidled up to them, cautious, alert, and he looked ahead, he looked sharply in the distance to where Fido lay with FEAR and PRIDE and HATE by his side. And he stopped. And he howled. Boris would come, too, but Paw and Princess and Sultan barked, and Feral gave a little yip that they would go to Fido, that it was for them, the last of the twelve disciples of NAV, to go to Fido, for they knew him, they loved him still, they had shared the love and scent of NAV. And Boris went back to stay with the humans and the dogs who were slowly shaking off their fear, stronger in the love of DOG.

Then with determination Feral stepped forth, he stepped to the edge of the Euphrates and he barked loud, so loud that none could believe, for none had ever heard him bark above a whisper. He barked that he would cross the river, that he and Paw and Princess and Sultan would cross the river to be with Fido. And the bark went out, and Fido left his place upon the dias in front of the palace and came to the edge of the Euphrates. He looked across, proud in the power of his followers, proud in his birth from NAV, filled with hate for all those who would not follow him. He looked across and he saw Paw and Princess and Sultan and Feral, and he knew them, and he was proud, they had come to him. They would recognize him. And he barked, "Where is Boris, the false DOGGY LAMA?" And Feral barked that he was with the humans and dogs back farther from the shore. That Boris would abide with whatever would come from their meeting. That it was for the first followers of NAV, those of the twelve disciples still breathing, to smell each other, to know the true way.

And FEAR and PRIDE and HATE at the side of Fido they were glad, for here were the last of the disciples of NAV. "Let them cross," they said in their screechy mewing voices. This was the great chance, the great chance for CAT to rule the world. These last disciples would acknowledge the true birth of Fido as the son of NAV, the true leader of dogs and humans, or they would die. "Let them cross," they mewed, and Fido turned, and the humans and dogs that followed him receded from the bank of the Euphrates to make room for these last of the disciples of NAV to cross.

Then slowly, with great effort, against the strong pull of the current, in the muddy waters, first Feral swam across. Then Princess and Paw and Sultan came, swimming close to each other, each careful the other should not falter, not drown in the fast and muddy current. They swam with all the strength they had left in their old bodies, strong in the love of DOG, strong in the hope of the love of Fido they would share.

They came to the bank of the river, first Feral stepping out and shaking himself. Then Paw, supported by Princess and Sultan, stepped out slowly, wincing in the pain of his hips and shoulders but happy in the reunion with Fido. He shook himself and turned to Princess and Sultan. Then they, too, raised themselves from the muddy waters, walking through the mud of the bank of the Euphrates, they came, they shook themselves and lay down. All lay down except Feral, who came closer to Fido, tail between his legs, whining. He came close, no threat, smelling strong from the wet fur, a smell that Fido remembered well from so long ago, the smell they shared at the side of NAV. He came closer, then suddenly stopped. His tail went up, erect, his head no longer lowered, his ears pointed up, his nose twitching and twitching. This was the moment he had prepared for all these many years, this was the reason he had been always alert, had prowled always the edge of camps, had hung back, had looked to the left and the right and behind but never putting himself in front. This he knew was the moment, for he smelled the stench of cat. He, who had trained so long to recognize what is catty in the world and to be prepared, he could not be deceived. He looked, and he smelled. And he smelled that PRIDE and FEAR and HATE were cats, the stench of the untanned hides they wore no deception to him. Feral growled softly, slowly, and Fido was angry, "Feral you came in peace and love, yet you growl." And Feral replied, "Yes, I growl, but not at you. I growl at these cats!" And he leapt forward, pointing with head and tail in a straight line looking at FEAR and PRIDE and HATE. He growled more strongly and then he barked. And then came up to him Paw and Princess and Sultan, and they looked. And though old, though their noses were weak, DOG made them strong and they could smell the stench of cat upon FEAR and PRIDE and HATE. And they growled. And Fido was angry, "These are my trusted advisers, they have led me here." And Feral barked a great bark that was the bark of the love of DOG, and joined him were Paw and Princess and Sultan in a great bark of the love of DOG, and lo, FEAR and PRIDE and HATE were afraid, for there was the love of DOG, so strong, the faith learned from NAV now confronting them in these last of the twelve disciples, old, but powerful in their love. And they stepped back. And lo, the untanned hides slipped away from them, and lo, the claws from their fingers came out, retracted so long, they came from what were now paws, and their tails could be seen, swishing, and they dropped to the ground on all fours, and the smell of CAT was great. And they screeched, "Kill them. Kill these false prophets of NAV. Only Fido is great, only Fido is the son of NAV. Kill them."

Then Fido knew that these were the cats of CAT, that they had led him to the way of CAT, for never could he kill these last of the twelve disciples of NAV, those who had loved him and loved him still. He turned, and barked, "Get thee behind me, CAT" and Feral and Princess and Sultan and even Paw in his great pain leaped at HATE and FEAR and PRIDE. And FEAR and HATE and PRIDE of the twelve cats of CAT, they screeched, "Kill them!" But now all could see that they were cats of CAT. Then FEAR and PRIDE and HATE ran, fleeing, and Feral and Princess and Sultan chased, while Paw, too old to run, came close to Fido and licked him and laid down at his side. Then returned Sultan and Princess and Feral, panting, for they were too old, too slow to catch FEAR and PRIDE and HATE who would continue to roam the world, always ready to be near humans and dogs who forget the way of love.

Others, the followers of Fido, the dogs and humans who had proclaimed Fido the Hidden One, the son of NAV, all the Sonnys now saw that it was CAT who had led them. And they were angry. They cried, "Fido is a false prophet. Fido has led us into the way of CAT. Kill Fido."

Then Sultan and Princess and Paw and Feral stood between them and Fido. They barked and barked until, swimming strongly across the river, came Boris, Boris from the north, from the Arctic Circle, the great hunter of wolves, his thick white hair matted with the muddy water, he swam swiftly, strongly, and came upon the bank of the Euphrates. He stood, he shook himself, and he looked at all. On the one side of him stood Fido, who had before him Feral and Paw and Princess and Sultan. And Fido knew that these four, the last of the disciples of NAV, would protect him with love but would never kill, they would die for him, but they would not kill. And on the other side of Boris, the crazed Sonnys, calling for blood. And Boris barked, "There is no crime so great that one cannot be redeemed in the love of NAV, redeemed to once more follow DOG in the way of peace and love. You cry and scream and bark that you were misled by Fido, but were not FEAR and HATE and PRIDE among you and did you not listen to them? FEAR and HATE and PRIDE are powerful, and you could not recognize them for you had no longer the love of DOG in your heart, the love that NAV brought us. And we, those who were strong in the love of DOG, we were content to teach and forgot the anguish of one of our own, the anguish of Fido who could not stand alone in the crushing loss of NAV."

Then Boris went to Fido, he came to him crawling on his belly, slowly crawling forward, then he cautiously stood and let Fido smell him and he licked Fido. And Fido could smell the sweet smell that is greater than the smell of death, a great smell, and he whimpered, and he let Boris smell him, and he licked Boris, and he howled and howled and howled.

Then all the Sonnys, all the humans and dogs who had been deceived into the way of CAT, were sore ashamed. They cried, they howled. But Paw and Princess and Sultan and yes, even Feral, went among them, they licked, they looked into their eyes, they comforted. And they all howled a howl of loneliness that could be assuaged only by love, a howl that turned into a sweet sense of all howling to one another, from near, from far, one, then another, all joined together howling back and forth, strong in the pack, the pack that would know that love has no pride, love has no fear, love has no hate. And from across the river, from those who had come with Boris and the last of the twelve disciples of NAV, came answering howls, not of loneliness but of love, howls that were clear and bright. And the humans called to one another, too, in their human kind of howl. They howled, all of them, they howled until they howled together in a great howl. And they rested. Then the once-Sonnys, the once-followers of Fido, went out to bring in meat and grain to cook. And those who had come with Boris and Paw and Princess and Sultan and Feral, they swam across the river, the river that had been so fast now only a trickle, so little, they swam and walked across, the many, the few, until as the last of the humans pulled herself out of the water, shaking herself, the Euphrates began once more to rush, a great river, flowing muddy and strong.

They would share the meat and grain, the greens, too, boiled and roasted on the fires, the fires they had learned to build from Prometheus, the bold, the strong, so tall, so strong, with massive jaws, full of life, short tan hair, large paws, he from the cold north of the Baltic Sea, from the forests and streams, Prometheus who was now gone, who had fallen to the claws of the twelve cats of CAT, yet who lived in the flow of all those who breathed now.

But Fido whimpered, he howled a mournful howl, he walked in circles. He could not be comforted. Paw came to him and laid down beside him, but Fido would not stop, his anguish greater still, fear still in his heart, for he had lost the love of NAV in his striving to be close to NAV, he deserved no love now from any dog or human. And Princess came close to Fido and licked him and whimpered, but Fido could not be comforted. Sultan, too, licked Fido, he walked with Fido in the great circles Fido walked, but Fido could not be comforted. Even Feral, who had gone to the edge of the camp, to the darkening dusk beyond the fires to search always for the scent of CAT, he came to Fido and barked softly,

"Where there is love, there is the way of life. NAV set before you life and death. Choose ye life that you may live." But Fido could not be comforted, he was the lowest, he had led his followers to kill. He deserved no love.

Then in the last light of the day, when the fires began to show in a yellow flickering the faces of the humans and the muzzles of the dogs, there at the side of Fido was a woman. Dressed in rags she stood, and none knew from whence she came. And she had on her the odor of a newly washed baby, the odor of a newly born puppy, an odor that Paw knew. And Paw had a terrible catch in his throat. He thought it was the time that he would pass beyond, for this, he knew was Maria, dressed in the same rags she had worn when she had welcomed NAV into the world, Maria, the foster-mother of NAV, she whom Paw had known so long ago. And Feral came up, the only other of the twelve disciples of NAV who had known Maria, and he was amazed, for here she stood, smiling sweetly, smelling of a newly washed baby and a newly born puppy, smelling of mother's milk, she who had passed so long ago, she who had lived a good life but had aged and died sweetly while caressing NAV, who had died while NAV was licking her, who had died when Paw and Feral had been at her side, comforting and learning from NAV that death was as natural as life and that we never die unless we should pass from the love of DOG. Here was Maria, sweetly smiling, and she came to Fido. She came to him and put her hand on his head, and she stroked him. And Fido became calm, he whimpered, and Maria stroked him again. Then she sat, there at the edge of the light from the fire, and she let Fido put his head in her lap, and she stroked him, and she sang, the same lullabies she had sung to NAV so long ago. She sang. She ate not, she smiled at all but she touched only Fido, stroking him, singing to him through the long night. And all were amazed, they ate quietly, they murmured one to one, dog to human to dog to human that Maria had returned, she the foster-mother of NAV, to bring the peace that passes all understanding to Fido. NAV in his great compassion saw the suffering of Fido, NAV who had been fostered by Maria, NAV had whimpered to DOG to allow Maria to return in shape and form and substance as before to comfort Fido, for only she, Maria, could bring the peace that would fill the heart of Fido. NAV could not do it, for Fido's heart was still in anguish for the loss of NAV and could not survive the loss of NAV again when He would depart. And all those in the camp, the humans and the dogs, they softly said, they softly barked, "Arfy Maria, foster-mother of NAV, bring us peace through love." And a sweet sleep descended on all, the sleep of peace that heals, for they were filled with love again and could sleep.

The moon rose, soon the light, and Fido whimpered no more. Fido lay in a peaceful sleep, the first sleep of peace he had known since the passing of NAV. Rosy-fingered dawn, and Maria was there no more, returned to the flow of all with NAV and DOG. Only the smell of a newly washed baby, of a newly born puppy, of mother's milk lingered. Then Fido awoke, abashed but not burdened, refreshed in the love of all who accepted him. Accepted, for Maria and Paw and Princess and Sultan and yes, even Feral, and Boris, too, had shown that there is no power like the forgiveness of love.

Then the humans blew upon the fires to make them strong again, and they roasted meat, and they ate, quiet, each unsure but hopeful. Then Feral, the quiet and cautious one, came to the fires, he yipped, he jumped up, he nuzzled a human, he play-bowed to a dog, he ran in a circle, he yipped, he jumped, and the humans smiled, the dogs joined Feral, even Paw, so old and crippled, they danced in a circle, each dog taking gently in his teeth the tail of the one in front, each human taking the hand of the one in front extending the other hand behind in a great circle, they twirled, they sang, they barked, they yipped, for there was joy again, the joy of the love that NAV has brought from DOG, NAV, DOG's only Puppy, the joy of love that is greater than FEAR, greater than PRIDE, greater than HATE, greater even than death.

They twirled, they sang, they yipped, they jumped, they broke apart and came together again in the joy of reuniting, of all being in the love of DOG together once more. Of the greatness of the power of love that NAV had taught them they rejoiced.

And in the distance, there in the distance a shrill mewing cry that only Feral now at the edge of the camp could hear, the sound of FERRATSI, "We are here. HATE and FEAR and PRIDE still roam the earth. Our time will come." And Feral barked a great growling bark, while the others danced in joy.

The Gift of Writing

Then there was only Sultan, the last of the twelve disciples of NAV, the last who knew NAV, who knew his scent, his lick, who had lain at the fire listening to NAV teach of the love of DOG. Only he was left of the twelve, all the others were gone, passed into the great flow of all. Ralph, with his purple coat, his look aslant and always joking, who had taught of love through laughter, was gone. And Birta, brown and black, who had loved and loved and been loved, who had helped humans grow into love, now her last place of breath was marked with a great stone. And Lady, all white and golden, long since passed to be with NAV and DOG. And Juney who had been the first DOGGY LAMA now gone in the warm embrace of Ursula, a dogwood tree above the place of her last breath. And Bidú, the great protector, Bidú with black and white fur flying wildly, giant that he was, with his square face, the pieces of him now resting in a cave, the entrance concealed with a great stone. And Spot, the father of Sultan, all white with a black spot on his brow, short hair, always jumping, ready always to spring against CAT, rested in the Cedars of Lebanon in the love he had given to Sultan and which he had given to so many. Fido, small, with curling tail, black and white and tan and red, all intense, Fido who had been deceived by the cats of CAT but who had returned to the love of DOG, Fido was gone, peacefully, having known the love of the last of the twelve disciples in his old age. And Prometheus, the bold, the strong, so tall, so strong, with massive jaws, full of life, short tan hair, large paws, torn by the cats of CAT he rested where a holy spruce grows in the cold rocks. And Princess, the lovely one, shaggy and black and horrible to look at until you saw her eyes and the love that flowed from them, her rat-like tail wagging, she who had gone to Fido in his anguish, now she, too, lost somewhere, none knew of the place of her last breath, but gone, all knew, for her scent was nowhere. And Paw, the gruff, the surly who hid his great heart behind his black, black short coat, from the fertile ground near the Ganges, a cigar in his mouth, drooling, sniffing, Paw had lived only a short time after the reuniting beyond the Great Schism, at last resting in peace near Fido, near Fido whom he had loved as he had loved all the disciples of NAV, as he had loved all the humans who had touched him, he rested, no pain, no suffering, he rested. And Feral, the wild one, unkempt, with head too big and paws too small, who had searched always for FERRATSI the mountain lion of CAT and the twelve cats of CAT, he who had brought the great rejoicing and love out of the horror of the Great Schism, Feral, now somewhere in the vast forests of India rested, his last place unknown, he had gone from the camp one night, searching, wary, alert, but never returned. All gone, all passed into the great flow. Only

Sultan now, the youngest of the twelve disciples, who had known NAV only when NAV was old, when NAV was mature in his teachings, only Sultan remained.

So Sultan told the stories he knew. The wisdom and teaching of NAV, and the wisdom and teaching of Juney, the First DOGGY LAMA, and the wisdom and teaching of Boris, the Second DOGGY LAMA, who must still breathe, he must, for none had come to say they must search for a new DOGGY LAMA.

And Sultan felt a great burden. All remembered the stories, passed from dog to dog, from dog to human, from human to dog, from human to human they passed, each careful to repeat what he had heard, to say exactly what she had heard, to bark precisely only the bark of NAV, of Juney, of Boris, the bark of DOG. But Sultan could hear the stories change. Feral now was called the magnificent one—Feral who looked askance at all, who slunk around the edge of every camp. And Lady, who had loved and only loved, who had helped humans find love, who had never barked, was now called a dog of wisdom. The stories, even the wisdom, were changing, a cough while barking, a word murmured instead of said distinctly, the stories, even the wisdom, were changing.

Sultan knew there was so little time, so little time before he, too, would be gone. So he gathered to him all his puppies, and their puppies, and their puppies unto the 43rd generation, those that still breathed, for Sultan had lived long, had lived now 814 years. And he gathered to him all the children, and the children of the children, and the children of the children of the humans he had loved. So many of those he had loved had passed, had joined Ralph and Birta and Lady and Paw and Juney and Bidú and Spot and Fido and Prometheus and Princess and Feral in the great flow of all with NAV and DOG. So many humans he had loved, he had given all his love, first Abraham, who had passed and with his passing a great suffering for Sultan, and then Rachel, and she had passed and with her passing a great suffering for Sultan. And Ezekiel, and Isaiah, until now there was only Isabel, old, gnarled, twisted with pain, her hand upon Sultan, Sultan's head in her lap, love, always love, unconditional love that knows no bounds but bounds beyond all to the joy of love. Love that brings suffering, for without suffering there can be no knowledge of the power of love. And Sultan suffered now, thinking of the humans he had loved. He whimpered.

So little time for Sultan to pass on what he knew, to make sure the stories, the wisdom were not lost. Boris, tall, white hair flowing, loping, strong, the hunter of wolves, the Second DOGGY LAMA, in the cold Arctic could tell what he knew, could leave his wisdom to be passed on by bark and word, but he was so far away. And he had not lived in the time of NAV, he had not known the scent of NAV, the wisdom that NAV barked. It was time for Sultan to tell once more all he knew, all he could remember, before the stories and the wisdom might be lost.

And they listened. One of the puppies of a puppy of a puppy, of the 42nd generation of Spot, she listened, and she felt a breath. A warm breath in her ear, a strong scent of a sweetness greater than the smell of death, a little lick at her ear. She turned but no dog was there. She turned again but no human was near. She closed her eyes and she sniffed, twitching her nose, she breathed deeply and she knew that this was the breath of NAV, of NAV who breathed into her ear the way of writing, for DOG would not let the wisdom and stories be lost, he would send NAV to the puppy of the 42nd generation of Spot, to Belinda. And Belinda knew. She barked. And all were startled, and the humans cried out "Hush. Hush. Sultan is barking the stories and wisdom." And the dogs yipped, and two came and nipped at her. But Belinda barked and barked loud, "Stop. For I shall make a record of all that is said." And they were bewildered. Had they not a record in their memories? Had they not told the stories and wisdom time and time again so none should forget? But Belinda barked again, Belinda, small, tiny paws, short hair, white and red, descended, too, from Fido, she barked again that they must stop.

And Sultan heard, he heard, and he knew the bark, the bark of olden times, the bark that would not be stopped, for it was a bark given by DOG. He said no more, waiting. And Belinda told the humans to gather mud, clay from the banks of the Euphrates, and to make it into rectangles, wet clay mixed with straw. They brought the clay and fashioned it into rectangles. These were tablets, she said, and they would preserve the wisdom of NAV and of Juney and of all those who had gone before. They put a tablet before Belinda, and she put her paw into the wet clay, and again her paw, and again her paw, and look, she said, a pattern. She placed her paw again, and the humans looked, the dogs looked, and yea, they could see the pattern—here, this was the word for love, and these paw prints, they were the sign of peace, and those were the sign of NAV, so strong in the clay. And they could see. And they could read. And the young dogs watched and learned to make the paw prints that signified. And the humans, the youngest, watched and learned to press with sticks into the wet clay to make marks that looked like paw prints, they made marks that signified. And they could write. And they could read.

Then the humans raised a great shout of joy. Then the dogs yipped and jumped, they felt the new power, the strength to remember in the marks on clay. Then Belinda showed them to take the clay tablets and heat them near the fire, a little, not much, to heat them until they became hard. And all knew that the bark of DOG, the bark of NAV, the wisdom of Juney should never be lost so long as a single dog, a single human could read and write.

Then Sultan barked greatly, he barked with joy, for he knew that the barks of NAV, the wisdom of Juney would be safe. So he continued, he barked more, and others barked what they knew, and the humans told the stories and wisdom they had learned. A great many tablets were filled with the marks of paws, with the writing that DOG had given them through NAV and the paw of Belinda. And Sultan was glad, he could rest; his journey now was at an end. He called Belinda to him and barked, "You are the First SCRIBE. Mark tablets with all you can. Then go to Boris, the Second DOGGY LAMA, go there and mark his wisdom in the prints of your paws. Travel and travel to learn all the stories and wisdom from those who remember. Then return and remain with Boris, the second DOGGY LAMA, and rest there, find your human there, the man or woman to whom you can give your love without condition, and write of love, of the power of love, of NAV who was DOG's only puppy, of Juney who was the first DOGGY LAMA and who loved us in her wisdom of love. And write, too, of CAT and her twelve cats all led by the horrible one FERRATSI the mountain lion, write of them, so all shall beware. Write. Write."

And Sultan barked more and more. He barked without rest and the puppies of the 42nd and 43rd generation of Spot, they marked the tablets with paw prints signifying his barks. He barked, did Sultan, not stopping for food, lapping water, with the hand of Isabel upon him, Isabel who could no longer see, who also would not take food. Until there came a time when he could bark no more, when he had told all the stories, when Isabel breathed into his ear, "It is time for us to rest. We have done all we can. It is time to rest. The young ones will carry now the bark of DOG." And she lay down beside Sultan, and Sultan nuzzled against her, and they breathed together, in union, panting at the last, as the young ones gathered around them. They rested then, strong in the love of DOG, strong in the love of each other, they rested and breathed no more.

The last who had known NAV, who had breathed his scent, who had licked NAV and been licked by Him, who had rested near His paws and heard His bark, was gone. But the bark, the stories and wisdom continue in the paw prints in the clay tablets.

Then the young ones were startled, for from Sultan and Isabel came a sweet smell, a scent stronger than the smell of death. And they looked, and they could no longer see Sultan, they could no longer see Isabel, they were gone, only their bark and words remained, only their love remained, there among them.

Then the humans cried out with joy, the dogs yipped and jumped, all danced, for the great moment was with them, the moment when Sultan and Isabel passed into the great flow of all. They danced, they shouted, they barked, they built a fire and roasted the meat with dripping fat, they ate, they danced again until they fell down exhausted, exhausted with the joy of love, full of the knowledge that love is greater than death.

Master Ts'en

There to the East, the East beyond where the land meets the sea, waves rolling on, waves rolling free, is the island where they eat rice and raw fish and seaweed. There at the farthest East, the bark of NAV was heard, the story of NAV, DOG's only Puppy, sent to live among us to teach all sentient creatures of love. There it was told of His Ascension on the first full moon after the Spring Equinox in his 911th year. Some barked, too, of Juney, the First DOGGY LAMA. They told the stories, the wisdom, one night, another night, parts, little, so little, and they yearned to hear more. The way of peace, of love that gives and shares, this they would learn.

Then came to them the story of Boris, the Second DOGGY LAMA, and the horror of the Great Schism, how FERRATSI, the horrible mountain lion who guides in the way of CAT through FEAR and PRIDE, the most horrible of all cats of CAT, had seduced Fido, Fido the faithful disciple of NAV, how they had with HATE led him and all near him to kill followers of DOG until Feral, the most wary of the disciples of NAV, had unmasked FEAR and PRIDE and HATE and with Boris led Fido back to the way of love.

This they heard, they tried to understand. Some parts were barked strangely, so far from where they had first been told. Each who carried the story would try to repeat it perfectly, but none are perfect, the stories traveled so far, the wisdom a little different every time. Feral, it was said, was wise. Bidú, it was said, had saved all at the Great Schism. Wrong, yet the spirit was there. The spirit, the great message that NAV brought to all who could learn, that, they felt, was sure, the message of the great way of love and peace that those who follow DOG try to learn and then to teach.

In that land where they eat rice and raw fish and seaweed lived a man, Ts'en. He went to the fields in the morning with the other villagers to plant rice, he sweated, he worked. Not tall, but strong enough he worked in the sun in the flooded fields where they planted the rice they had started in small baskets. With his young wife Shizuka, small, pretty, he worked each day. Now three years married, with a great love. She always happy to be with him, touching, still almost shy, they lived in the love of each other. Her long black hair wrapped under her straw hat, his back bare, glistening with sweat in the sun, they worked. No children, not yet, but they were not worried. Their love was so great, it was enough.

Then returning home at dusk from the fields they heard a horse, a great neighing and hooves trampling on the road behind them, then on them. Ts'en pushing

Shizuka aside, fast, he pushed her, and the horse came across his leg, trampling, his leg, now crushed. Great pain. He howled. Others came to him, came to look, to help, Shizuka crying, screaming for help. But there was nothing they could do. The leg was broken, crushed, they could only carry Ts'en home. For many days he suffered, great pain, with Shizuka always caring, always wiping his forehead with a wet cloth, holding his hand, never leaving, neighbors bringing a little rice, a little fish, some seaweed.

Ts'en's leg began to heal, he leaned upon a stick to walk, little by little he could walk. But never could he work in the fields again. Never again, the pain, unsteady in flooded paddies, he could only look as Shizuka planted, as Shizuka pulled weeds. At the end of the summer he watched as she brought in the little they had from the harvest, the little rice. So much work, not enough time. She worked, she became thin, and then thinner. Ts'en carried what he could, he tended what he could, he cooked, he cleaned, but he could not do the hard work of the fields. It was not possible. And Shizuka grew thinner. Then in the cold of the winter, the wind cold, the small hut so cold, only a little wood for a fire, Shizuka began to cough. She coughed one day, a thick watery cough. Another day. And Ts'en went out to his neighbors, begging, a little rice, a little broth. They gave, a little, for they too had not much, the harvest had been poor. He returned. The cough now thicker, watery. And on the fourth day Shizuka died.

Ts'en then began to moan. He moaned and moaned. He would not eat. The villagers comforted him. One talked to him of DOG and of the way of love and peace. He could not hear. They brought him a little rice and raw fish. He would not eat. He had no way in the world. He suffered.

Then again the message of love and peace, the way of DOG. To give, always to give without counting, this is the way, he was told. To give, and through giving to pass beyond suffering. He suffered, they said, but he could give to others.

Each day he thought, he ate a little. Yes, to give, to walk—crippled as he was in body and spirit—in the way of love and peace. To go beyond suffering. He meditated. He thought long and long. Suffering is the work of CAT, he had heard. It is not real. He meditated, seated on the earth, his good leg crossed over his crippled leg, lost in his thoughts, focussed on the distance. We suffer only as we see ourselves in hardship, without giving. To give of ourselves, that overcomes suffering. Unreal, all is unreal. Suffering is unnecessary, unreal.

78   The BARK of DOG

Ts'en meditated, and he began to count his breaths, one, two, three, four, five, six, seven, eight, nine, ten, eleven, twelve, . . . but he found his mind wandering, pictures of children he never had, of dogs, of cats, he found his mind wandering. Then he counted his breaths one, two, three, four, five, six, seven, eight, nine, ten, and lest he begin to wander in his thoughts, he began again, one, two, three, four, five, six, seven, eight, nine, ten, and he continued. Focussing on the distance, alert, aware, his hands on his knees as he sat with his good leg crossed over his crippled one, palms up, he breathed and counted. And his mind cleared. Not to become vacant, but to become open. Open to all, to pass beyond suffering to the great openness of all.

Now he learned: we can pass through suffering through the practice of meditation, of clarity, of each moment being a learner, having a beginner's mind, open to all. This is the way to love and giving, he thought, to be open, to see the unreality of good and evil, to practice non-attachment to the good and non-attachment to the bad. Not attached to what seems worth wanting, not even to the memory of Shizuka; not attached to the fear of what brings pain, not even to his crippled leg.

Ts'en meditated. Clear. He walked—though still crippled—more upright. The pain he did not notice, it was there, but so was the song of the birds in the trees, so was the rock in the road, so was the smile, and so was the harsh word the man called out to his ox. All was there, not real, for only the great flow of love was real, the flow we can perceive as we meditate, he said.

He walked more upright, without sorrow, open to all. He passed through suffering as he passed through the good that came to him. He would teach, he said, he would teach this way of non-attachment, the way of peace and love through non-attachment. It was his duty.

He met others, all struck by his peace and clarity. Those who knew his story were amazed that he had passed through the suffering. And he passed, too, through the awe that some held for him. Open, this he taught, we must be open. Non-attachment. He taught:

    This, too, shall pass.

He said this when the woman came to him in sorrow that her child had died: This, too, shall pass. He said this when the villagers came to him celebrating the great harvest: This, too, shall pass. Bad. Good. All unreal. Only the great flow of all. The great joy is being open in non-attachment. And this, he taught, we can learn through meditation. Not meditating to be closer to DOG, to be closer in spirit, but to be open to all, to the stars, to the mud, to the birds, to the maggots, to the flowers, to the rank weeds, open to all, all part of the great flow of love that DOG has given us.

Then many followed him. Master Ts'en they called him. They learned to meditate. They brought him rice and fish, clear water and seaweed. He ate little, they all shared. A community of those who would be good through the clarity they gained in meditation. Good they would be in the way of non-attachment, DOG's way, they said.

He walked among them as they meditated in the grove of pines, straightening this one's back, straightening that one's leg, flicking this one's ear to see if she would lose her focus. Discipline, he said, discipline is necessary to meditate. He became more harsh, loving but harsh to lead to more love. Discipline to meditate to finally achieve clarity and the ability to accept all and to give.

The calling of the crows he listened to. One crow to another. He interpreted them to his followers as puzzles, these crow-ons. To learn to think outside the circle, to think without thinking. They discussed "What is the sound of one tail wagging?" They considered "There is more than one way to skin a cat." They discussed the story of the man who would dress as a woman dressed as a man and whether there was a man or a woman in his or her actions. The crow-ons led them to be more open, to see more possibilities, to think outside the circle.

They meditated, and some became clear. Then more. They would not suffer, nor would they be seduced to be attached to the good that passes before them. They would give freely of themselves to all.

In the North, the most North of the islands there in the East beyond the limits of land where the sea begins, waves rolling on, waves rolling free, was a land of hairy people. There lived Akita, a hairy dog, husky, broad-shouldered, lumbering in his walk, his paws solid under his broad chest, grey with black and white, fur so thick. The North, where there were few humans, and Akita young, no human for him yet, so few there. He heard from others around the fire of the great love that NAV, DOG's only Puppy had come to teach. He learned a little of the way of DOG, of peace and love, and giving. He yearned to have a human he could love, for surely that is what was meant. But he was not worthy. He must learn of love. He must learn. Then he heard, from a small brown dog that had come from the South, of a way of meditation, of non-attachment leading to the way of love. He heard of the great Master Ts'en. And he would go.

80 The BARK of DOG

From the North came Akita, trotting South, he must know more, he must learn this great way of love and peace. Of the many smells in the world he knew little, he was young, he would go South, somehow to the island of the South. The barks told him of the great Master Ts'en, and he would learn.

Akita trotted, he trotted, his paws sore from rocks and the spray of the sea, he trotted always South until he could travel no farther, only the sea and in the distance another great island. So far, so far, yet he must go. He did not think, he did not stop, he leapt wide into the sea, paddling, farther and farther, away from the island of his home, farther to the great island of the South. The sun setting, the wind now calm, he paddled on and on, never stopping, not cold, not hot, only paddling. And on the next morning he came to the island to the South. He came to the beach, a great wave pushing him onto the sand, clear sand. He heaved in his breathing, he staggered, he fell, and he slept.

Farther he would travel, farther South to the land of the teacher of wisdom. He trotted, drinking from the little streams that go into the sea, catching a rabbit for nourishment, he trotted South.

He came to a village by the sea, and there he found a clearing in a grove of pines. He saw many men and women sitting cross-legged on the pine needles, staring out. So strange: he could see they were still, so still, only a man, a cripple leaning on a stick standing and looking, almost supervising the stillness. Akita would come forward, but he had nothing, nothing to offer. He ran off, and returned with a rabbit, bloody in his mouth. He came forward slowly to the man standing, supervising all this stillness. He came, and he waited until those who sat cross-legged stretched, got up, began to talk slowly, and he put before the man the rabbit. The man smiled, he petted Akita, and showed the rabbit to those who meditated. Tonight they would have meat in the broth, an offering.

Each day Akita came to the clearing, watching. The man, now Master Ts'en Akita knew he was called, helped him. He taught him to lie with paws in front, head erect, counting his breaths, one, two, three, four, five, six, seven, eight, nine, ten, and then starting again. Akita, there in the back, counting, his mind becoming clear. But so many smells! The sea and the grass and the forest nearby with trees in blossom, the cherry trees and the rabbits, the little mice, so many smells! Akita focussed ahead, breathing, his mind not yet clear, his thoughts wandering, not yet open, he knew not yet fully the path of giving and sharing. He would learn. He had love in his heart, and here he would learn the sure way to fix it there. He had no human, he had only a sense of love, but that would come later, when he was clear and peaceful as these followers of Master Ts'en, then he might have a human.

He would learn to meditate, he would learn the crow-ons. Yet he would fidget, biting the fleas, and he would look yearningly at the hills with new grass and whiff with yearning the scent of the new grass and the rabbits. Then Master Ts'en would tap him, would tap him, and Akita would start and once again take the posture, breathing one, two, three, four, five, six, seven, eight, nine, ten, one breath on each count, then again, one, two, three . . . continuing and continuing. He must learn, he must learn the way of love through clarity of mind. He had not yet learned of non-attachment, that all was illusion, that suffering was an illusion we are led to by CAT, that there is no self but only the great flow of all.

Akita looked at Master Ts'en lovingly, so wise. Akita's focus not clear, his thoughts still seduced by attachment to good and to bad. He meditated. No! No focus, he thought. I will try again. Focus! Clarity. But he turned his head to the hills again. And he saw on the road leading past the clearing a little girl walking by, and he knew his place was with her. Akita did not stop, he ran to the little girl, licked her, nuzzled close to her. The little girl cried, afraid, then Akita nuzzled more, crouching, and she touched him, she petted him, she stroked Akita's heavy dark fur, and she laughed. Then Akita licked her again, and again. She ran off with Akita bounding behind, around, in front, barking and yipping, returning again and again to be petted, chasing all who might be a danger. The mother of the little girl, a little way behind, at first crying, afraid of the great hairy dog. Then smiling as she came closer, seeing the child and the great hairy dog playing, running, Akita licking the little girl, the mother then content, petting Akita, Akita happy for the petting but attached only to the little girl. This, he knew, was the human he would give all his love to. This one. A human for him, he knew, and the mother kindly. They went off, the three of them, the mother happy, for the child had no father, no man, her man now long gone in a boat fishing, never returning. Akita, so loving, so careful, guarding the little girl, the mother was happy. Now a family.

After many days, three moons, Akita returned to the clearing, the little girl playing with him, tugging at his ears, running. And Akita barked to those in the clearing, "Unconditional love." Then again, "Unconditional love, this is all, this is the way of DOG." He ran off, to protect the little girl, barking, bounding.

Another moon, a clear day, the mother and the little girl walking to the market on the road that passes the clearing in the pines, where sat many meditating.

The little girl ahead, Akita running behind, around, nuzzling her, sniffing for danger, alert, loving. They passed the clearing, and Akita could hear Master Ts'en leading the Ts'en Dogists in talk of a crow-on, and Akita, so happy, he barked, "Unconditional love—it is not possible with non-attachment. Clarity is not the way, only unconditional love." And as he barked, bow-wowing to them, the little girl ran in front, ran ahead on the road, and coming from the other direction, swiftly, a horse, galloping, galloping, neighing, wild, frothing, running, running down the path, and far behind a man yelling, "Stop. Stop." Galloping, and the little girl in the road. Akita hears, he looks up, the little girl now far ahead, the horse galloping, frothing. Akita barks, the little girl looks up, the horse runs on, striking her with its great hooves, striking her, she yelps, a short gagging cry. And she lies still. Akita running to her. Crumpled, crushed. Akita nudges her, not believing. He nudges her again. No movement, no breath, the smell of death. His love, his human, to whom all love is due, she is dead. Akita howls, he howls and he howls. He will not stop.

The mother screams, she screams at Akita, running to them, she kicks Akita, kicks at him, her baby dead, Akita not guarding, distracted. Akita, trust betrayed, Akita barking at those in the clearing, now her baby dead.

Akita slinks to the side, he slinks, sorrow overcoming, no howling, only guilt. Guilt—he should have been at her side, he could have barked, pushed her aside, flung himself at the horse. Better he should have died, not her, his loved one. But he had stopped to hear of non-attachment. Guilt. He lay down, the mother now howling, crying, flinging herself on the ground, the little girl lifeless.

Then a voice came to Akita, a small breath in his ear. He looked. No one. No dog, no human near him, him the one of guilt. Then the small bark in his ear.

> She is gone, but she is in the flow of all, the love that sustains us, the flow we are part of. She is there through your love, you taught her to love. And you taught her mother to trust. Guilt—No. GUILT is one of the cats of CAT, the hidden one, masked as responsibility. GUILT is the poison of love.
>
> Unconditional love. Suffering leads to deeper love, but perverted it leads to guilt and death.

The followers of Master Ts'en rushed to them, hurried to the little girl, the mother, comforting her. Master Ts'en limping behind came to Akita, came in gentleness and kindness. He touched Akita, for Akita suffered, Master Ts'en came to him with compassion to speak of non-attachment. That suffering is an illusion, that we must let go of the illusion. That we can walk in peace and love only if we clear our minds of the illusion of separateness, of the reality of suffering. The others gathered, they were sad for Akita, but they knew his suffering was not real, it was only his perception that was suffering, his perception, his wanting that misled him. They were sad for the mother, but they knew her suffering was not real, it was only her perception that was suffering, her perception, her wanting that misled her. She, the little one, is gone but she is not gone.

Akita trembled. He knew he had heard the bark of DOG. He crept to the little girl, he crept to her, he let the mother kick him, he whined, and the mother calmed. He lay there, the mother hit him again, not so hard, and he licked her hand, he lay next to the little girl. He nuzzled to the mother who hit him again, not so hard, and Akita licked her hand and nuzzled closer to her. The mother could not hit again. She could not. She took Akita in her arms and cried into the heavy thick fur at his neck. She cried and she cried. She knew how much Akita had loved the little girl, how much he had taught the little girl—and her. She hugged him. She cried. He nuzzled to her, whining.

And Master Ts'en talking of non-attachment, of how he was crippled because of his leg, but that he did not suffer, that his wife Shizuka was gone, but he did not suffer. And the mother wailed again. Master Ts'en touched her, told her of non-attachment, that suffering is not real.

Then Akita rose up and barked so that all could understand, all the men, all the women, all the dogs, so that all could understand in their hearts, as if the bark were within them:

> Not non-attachment but love, unconditional love, love that will as surely lead to suffering as to peace.
>
> Not to avoid suffering. To avoid suffering is selfish, but to love, to give and give, not selflessly but of yourself, to love deeply and, yes, perhaps to suffer.
>
> Not to avoid suffering but to learn. What you do with the suffering, that is what matters, that is what can lead to love, to follow with love.
>
> To see death as part of the flow and to continue to love. It is what you do with the suffering that makes your life.
>
> It is better to have loved and lost than never to have loved at all.

The humans listened. Master Ts'en, who had so long struggled to find the way, through discipline and clearing the mind, he listened. The humans who had sat so many hours in the perfect posture, they listened. Many dogs heard, too, turning and rubbing one against another, sniffing.

    Not to suffer is not to live.

    Not to suffer is to walk through life as a sleepwalker,
    giving yet empty of desire, empty of aversion. Empty.

And Master Ts'en cried, he cried, he cried, remembering his Shizuka, the loss, his leg and pain, his loss, for the first time in so many years he cried, he howled. He crept closer to Akita. On his crutch slowly he came to Akita. He bows, deeply, more deeply, he falls to his good knee, his crippled leg behind, then throws his crutch on the ground and puts his head in the dust before Akita. He cries, and he calls, "Akita, my master." And Akita licks him, bowing to him, no master, no follower, licking Master Ts'en behind the ear, Master Ts'en tickled, his great silence in the posture of bowing broken as he brushes at his ear, then licking again, and the great master smiles, he smiles, he lives again.

Then a sweet smell arose, a sweet smell stronger than the smell of death came from Akita and flowed over the little girl. There, certain of her love and the flow of love of all Akita jumped up, face still twisted in sorrow but now cocked to the side as if listening, as if listening to the great flow of all rushing past and through him and through all.

They came to the little girl, they all touched her, she who had led Akita who had led them to learn of love, of unconditional love. They touched her, they wept, the mother of the little girl wailing as Akita drew close to her, nuzzled against her, licking her. Master Ts'en, now only Ts'en, touched the little girl and smelled the sweet smell that is stronger than the smell of death.

They took the little girl, the mother carrying her, to the grove of trees by the road, the humans digging there with their hands, the dogs with their paws scratching at the earth. The mother now easier, placing her darling in the ground, then throwing earth upon her, there, the little girl who had taught of love more than any meditation. The humans taking the mother's hands, circling with her. Akita always at her side, around they circled, the humans calling, the dogs barking, in a great circle of love, sustaining through the suffering. Then a small boy, one who could only begin to understand, he ran off, a little girl with him, a small brown dog following, returning with a new rice plant they brought to

Master Ts'en. He looked, Akita led him to the earth covering the little girl, and dug a little. Master Ts'en, no longer master, only Ts'en, fell to his good knee and planted there the rice shoot, green, so green. The little boy and the little girl running off, returned with water in a small jug, and each man, each woman dropped a little on the dark earth, a little more, another jug of water, more and more, then the dogs, coming to the plant, each making a single drop of water, caressing the earth and the little girl beneath the earth with their water of love. And the green shoot began to grow, it grew, not big but beautiful, and it is still there, so many years, so many dog-years, ever green, it grows with the love of the Little Girl, the Saint who leads to love through suffering.

Then Akita led to dance. A great circle, each dog taking gently in his teeth the tail of the one in front, each human taking the hand of the one in front extending the other hand behind in a great circle, they twirled, they sang, they barked, they yipped, for there was joy again, the joy of the love that NAV has brought from DOG, NAV, Dog's only Puppy, the joy of love that is greater than GUILT, greater than death.

They had learned. They had learned. There, by the sea in the grove of pines, they built a great fire, four dogs went out and returned with a deer, a deer the humans placed above the fire. They sat as the meat roasted, fat dripping into the flames, quiet, sad but deep in their love. They sat as they ate, each giving to another, none taking until all had meat, all could eat of the sacrifice of the deer as the child, the little girl, had sacrificed so they would learn of love.

Then to the clearing came an old one, a dog so old he could walk only slowly, jerking in pain, easing himself, late, he came and they gave him meat, they chewed it for him, his eyes not seeing. A wolf-hunting dog he was, one who had been with Boris, the Second DOGGY LAMA so long ago, so many dog-years now, more than a hundred, he guessed. He sat with them, he listened. Then he sniffed, and sniffed again, pricking up his ears. He looked with eyes that could not see. He walked to each and smelled each, and passed by Master Ts'en, by the followers of Ts'en, until, quivering, shaking in all his body as if he were to fall, he howled, a great howl of joy as he touched Akita, as he smelled the sweet smell he knew from long ago at the side of Boris, the Second DOGGY LAMA. Then he knew that Boris had gone, he was no more, Boris had joined in the great flow with NAV and with Juney, for the sweet smell had passed to Akita. And the old white wolf-dog jumped—all were amazed, he jumped, so old, and he ran, haltingly, barking, yipping that here, here was Akita, the Third DOGGY LAMA.

Exodus

From out of the desert land near the Middle Sea came the Twelve Cats of the Apocalypse, came HATE, GREED, VENGEANCE, LUST, GLUTTONY, PRIDE, IMPATIENCE, INDIFFERENCE, SLOTH, SCHADENFREUDE, GUILT, and ALLERGY, all led by FEAR, the most powerful cat of CAT, she who answered only to FERRATSI, the mountain lion, who answered only to CAT. They came, conquering all, mewing and screeching, clawing and biting, across many lands, conquering in the name of CAT, killing all who would not bow to CAT, who would not accept the way of CAT. And the small cats, the little followers of the Twelve Cats of the Apocalypse, they came, too, fornicating, screeching, killing songbirds, making many kittens, one litter, then another, then another, and there was a great stench of CAT upon the world.

And FEAR taught humans to kill in the name of CAT, to conquer with her, to destroy all who would not bow to CAT. So when they came to a camp of followers of DOG, to a village or gathering, even to a town, the humans fell upon the followers of DOG, they struck and bit, and the followers of DOG would not fight. No, they would not kill a human, not kill a dog. They offered only love, the love that is greater than death, knowing that though they may die they would live in the flow of love. And they died, many, men and women, dogs and bitches, children and puppies, they died in the villages in the mountains, in the oases in the desert, in the cold camps in the North, in the towns by the sea. Many died, and the human followers of DOG were few, and the dogs were almost none.

They would not fight, they would not kill, they would offer only love. But they did not stay to be slaughtered. From the North, from the South, from the East, from the West, they traveled to the mountains near the Middle Sea, to the cedars of Lebanon where Spot had once taught of the love of DOG, where Sultan the puppy of Spot had learned to love and to give all in unconditional love. They gathered there in the sacred place, continuing to practice the way of DOG, the way of love. They did not pray, for they knew that prayer was only fear and want, they knew that better than prayer was to live in the way of DOG, giving and loving. They did not fear, but they were careful.

Then came the many cats, the cougars and the lions and the tigers. They had found this last hidden place of Spot and Sultan, they had found the only remaining followers of DOG, the only humans and dogs who knew of unconditional love.

And the many cats and the cougars and the lions and tigers screeched and clawed, and the followers of DOG fought them, for they would not spare a cat. The followers of DOG were strong in their faith and in their arms and in their jaws. Then SLOTH, one of the Twelve Cats of the Apocalypse, a fat tabby cat of CAT, striped with tail swishing, he called to the many cats and the cougars and the lions and the tigers in his ugly mewing screech to withdraw and let the humans, the humans who acknowledge CAT, go first.

And though the followers of DOG would fight the cats, the cougars and the lions and the tigers, they would not harm a human. They would offer only love, unconditional love, turning their cheeks, their muzzles, for better it is to die than to kill a human or dog. And the humans who worshipped CAT laughed, and pushed the followers of DOG into a corral, into a camp to concentrate them to the wish of SLOTH.

Then came SCHADENFREUDE, a great one of the Twelve Cats of CAT. She told her humans to take one from the concentration camp. And they took Leonardo, a large husky dog, heavy grey fur, white chest, curled tail, panting. And they held him. And Leonardo would not fight, for these were humans, he could not kill nor even bite. And SCHADENFREUDE screeched that they should tear him apart, tear him piece by little piece, a paw, a part of his tail, his nose they cut, and Leonardo would not fight. No, nor would he whimper. Only as they began to cut out his heart, he barked the bark that Prometheus had taught them so long ago, "Blessed be DOG and His only Puppy that I am grateful for the life you have given me. Father, NAV, I come to thee." And the followers of DOG, the few remaining, gathered, concentrated in the horror of the camp, they were strong in the love of DOG, and they feared not.

Then SCHADENFREUDE screeched that the followers of DOG were weak, that the humans and dogs were weak, they would not fight, they were cowards, dogs, humans, good only for the pleasure of seeing them suffer. And she mewed, and the many cats and the cougars and the lions and the tigers all growled happily, and the humans who followed CAT laughed. For they were strong. They could kill.

Then SCHADENFREUDE told the human followers of cat to guard the followers of DOG until the morning, when they would torture another, then another, until there would be no more. There, in this concentrated camp the humans who follow DOG and the last dogs would be exterminated so that no sign, no scent, no memory of DOG would survive on earth. The last dogs were to be skewered, roasted to be feasted on, and the humans cut into pieces to be fed to cats. Then the fierce humans who followed CAT, loyal to the Twelve Cats of CAT, being HATE, GREED, VENGEANCE, LUST, GLUTTONY, PRIDE, IMPATIENCE, INDIFFERENCE, SLOTH, SCHADENFREUDE, GUILT, and ALLERGY, and supremely FEAR, guarded the fence around the camp, the fate of the last followers of DOG now sure.

They did not know, these cats of CAT, they were blinded in the reek of CAT, that love, unconditional love comes to each of us, that every human has the power of love, and though all dogs might die, the lesson of love they taught would be learned again and again by humans. Already, in the mountains of the cedars of Lebanon, in the fertile land of the Ganges, even in the desert hills north of the land Aztechoia where Tiny had taught the love of DOG, in places no cat would find, the followers of DOG had hidden golden tablets marked with the Bark of DOG, the tablets with the stories and wisdom printed in paw marks, so the wisdom of love would not die.

Rosy-fingered dusk drew on, the red in the clouds speaking of the heart of DOG to the humans and dogs in the camp. Darkness grew. Though they knew that they were to die, that they would suffer, they knew, too, that to suffer for love is the greatest any dog or human can do. They were not afraid. Then from among them came a small bark, a small bark from a very small dog, small with tan and white silky hair, only a little more than a puppy, came a bark. And she barked again, did Lily, "Know me, Oh my DOG, know me, that I love Thee still, and though these who follow CAT are hateful it is only through FEAR and PRIDE they rule. Though they reek of cattiness, still shall I love them, for all creatures can be made good through love." And the others, though knowing their last time was near, they cried out and barked, "Know me, oh my DOG, that I follow thee in the way of NAV, of love, and I shall have no hate in my heart, but only love, only unconditional love."

And the cats that heard were uneasy, they screeched, for the sounds of the barks and the cries of the dogs and humans were sweet, and they might lead the humans who followed CAT away from the path of CAT. They screeched, but the followers of DOG, they sang and howled with great joy, for if they were to die it would be in the love of DOG, and as they gave love so would they live forever in the great flow of love.

Then came a scent to the last human followers of DOG, to the last dogs on earth, a scent stronger than the smell of death, a smell both sweet and doggy, a scent first slight, then more. And they knew that NAV was among them, NAV the only Puppy of DOG. Though they would die, though they would suffer, NAV was near to draw them to him in love. And they rejoiced, they cried and whimpered, they called out and barked, they danced. And the humans who guarded the camp were amazed. Here were humans and dogs who knew they would die, who knew they would suffer, and they were dancing, they were singing. And the humans who followed DOG, and the dogs, they came to the fence and offered love, they sang and they touched, though their paws had been crushed by heavy clubs, though their hands had been crushed by heavy clubs, they would not cry nor whimper, but offered only love.

And the humans who had gone the way of CAT were amazed. They knew that they had the greatest power, the power to torture and to kill, yet these followers of DOG were not afraid. They had a strange power, a power that those who followed CAT had forgotten, for all are born with the power of love, and it is only through the work of CAT that we forget. And they cried, for they, too, would love and be loved. They wanted, not yet knowing that loving is to give, but wanting love. Their hearts were full and sad, and they listened to the songs of the humans and the sweet howls of the dogs, the songs and howls that NAV had given them through his disciples, through Ralph and Birta, through Lady and Paw and Juney, through Bidú and Spot and Fido and Prometheus, through Princess and Sultan, and, yes, even through Feral. The songs and wisdom of the heart that the DOGGY LAMAS had passed to them, these they knew, and they sang, and they shared, and the catists, the humans who reeked of the scent of CAT, accepted, they touched the hands of the human followers of DOG, they stroked the heads of the few dogs, and they learned of love.

Then came a terrible screeching, a horrible screeching from the many cats, the cougars and the lions and the tigers who had found this last hidden place of Spot and Sultan, who had found the only remaining followers of DOG, the only humans and dogs who knew of unconditional love. They screeched and roared as they saw the human followers of CAT changing. And lo, though the humans had followed CAT for so long, yet the scent of CAT was no longer upon them, they were clean, they could smell the sweet and doggy scent of NAV, and they would be one with Him. And the Twelve Cats of the Apocalypse were furious, they screeched and roared, they would not be cheated of this chance to exterminate the last followers of DOG, the last dogs, so that no sign, no scent, no memory of DOG would survive on earth.

The humans who guarded the fence, they opened the gate. Though afraid, for they had not learned fully how to love, they were willing. And the followers of DOG came out, led by Lily, so small, with tan and white silky hair, only a little more than a puppy, she led, yipping lightly, "All who love DOG, follow me." And they walked and trotted out. Then the many cats, the cougars and the lions and tigers fell upon them, tearing and biting. And of the Twelve Cats of the Apocalypse, VENGEANCE and HATE and PRIDE and IMPATIENCE attacked, then followed FEAR and GREED and LUST and GLUTTONY and INDIFFERENCE and SLOTH and SCHADENFREUDE and GUILT. Even ALLERGY, she, too, attacked, and the followers of DOG, all the humans there and the few remaining dogs, they fought these cats that would proclaim the way of CAT. They bit, they tore, they clubbed their way through them, they fought with the great faith of love knowing that to kill one of the Twelve Cats of the Apocalypse would be good, would help all who would follow to lead a dogly life. But they could not kill these cats of CAT, they could barely pass through the many cats, the cougars and the lions and the tigers, until they were past them, they were in the valley beyond the valley where Spot had once taught of the love of DOG, where Sultan the puppy of Spot had learned to love and to give all in unconditional love. The humans and the few remaining dogs plunged ahead, in the dark, and lo, though there had been no moon, now there was the light of a full moon, light that showed a path. And Lily yipped, "Smell ye, smell the scent of NAV, he leads us." And they followed, hurrying, worried not for life but that too few of them would last to carry on the Bark of DOG. And a mist came up, small water hovering in the air, and the cats of CAT could not follow, they could not see nor smell the way of the followers of DOG, as they could not see nor smell the way of DOG.

The followers of DOG walked and trotted, they walked and trotted strong in the faith of DOG, in the love they shared, teaching those who had followed CAT of the love that is stronger than death. They came then out of the mountains of the cedars of Lebanon into a great desert. They walked on, but the grey and sandy desert offered no shelter from the heat, no water, no grain nor milk nor rabbits to sustain them. They walked, panting, their lips dry, they walked until on the second day they saw in the distance an oasis, a mirage it seemed, but as they walked it grew closer and closer. And it was an oasis, the oasis of Kelev Tov, the oasis from whence had come Juney, the sweet, the peaceful, the joyful, who was the First DOGGY LAMA. They came to the oasis, and they found there all the humans, all the dogs slaughtered, their bones white in the sun. But they found there, too, date palms, they found there fig trees, and olive trees, and they found clear water, a clear spring. Though there was little water, they shared, and lo, there was more water, and the figs they ate were not the last for new ones grew as they watched. And they ate and drank. And there were rabbits, one, then another, then another, so each dog could eat.

Then they would stay there, some said and others barked, "Let us stay here and grow old in the love of DOG. DOG through NAV has granted us this place, let us stay." Then Lily, small and silky, only a little more than a puppy, she yipped, "Yes, grow old in your greed, in your fear, in your sloth and indifference. No, this is the way of CAT, to rest here. We must continue to a greater land with many humans, where we shall show the love of DOG. We shall go there, to the promised land, which shall be known as Dogistan, there to grow and multiply and share." And they were ashamed, were they all, especially those who had followed CAT for they knew especially of the power of the cats of CAT called GREED, SLOTH, INDIFFERENCE, and most terribly FEAR.

So the next day they walked and trotted on, led by Lily, the small silky one, always East and North, to the great steppes of the North, they walked in the desert. They walked, and though they were hungry, they would not eat the grain they had brought with them in the small bags they carried, for this was the hope of the future, the seeds they would sow for a new life where NAV would lead them. And every second day at rosy-fingered dusk they came to an oasis with a little water, a fig tree and a date tree and a few rabbits so they could survive.

Then they came to a great ridge of mountains, high, rocky, from the South and West to the North and East there were only mountains, steep, craggy, and they could not find a way. Then Lily, the small and silky one, not larger than a puppy, she yipped, "I smell the way. There, NAV leads us on." And they followed and found a high pass. They descended the mountain, the rocks with no path, they descended into a land of much green. A land of green, then more green, and great trees, and great ferns, and green growing everywhere. But nothing for them to eat. It rained. And it rained. And it rained. A land where there was mud, where there was no path, where each step sloshed, and the water was not clean to drink. It rained a cold rain, colder than any they had felt. They were weak. Yet none would blame Lily, no, whether she had truly caught the scent of NAV or whether she had been mistaken, they would not blame, for that is the way of CAT. Though they were cold, no sun, no wood dry enough for a fire, no fruit nor rabbits, they walked and humbly offered the little they had to each other. Until there was nothing more to share except their love, no fruit nor meat, no clean water, only the grain in their sacks that they would not touch, for they had faith that they would sow it one day in the promised land.

Then Lily, the small and silky one, not larger than a puppy, found a clearing, a place with no trees, no ferns, only mud, slippery, black mud. She stopped. She barked, and she barked again, "Oh NAV, is this the place?" And she barked to them, "Take from your sacks, you humans, the grain that you have brought, the seeds that we have for the time when we shall be in the land to which NAV is leading us, take the grains we have brought for our new life and sow them here."

Many doubted, many hesitated. There was only mud. There was no sun to grow, and even if the grain should grow, the barley and wheat, how could they mill it and cook it when the wood on every side was so wet it could not burn? But Lily barked, "This is the way, here we shall survive."

And Lily barked again, "Plant here. DOG giveth." Then they had faith and planted the seeds. And the next day the sun shone brightly, steam rising from the earth, warm, a great sun. And the grain grew, yes in one day it grew great and matured and was ripe. And on the second day they heard the bleating of a goat, a giant goat, bigger than the biggest dog, twice the height of the biggest human, it strolled slowly into camp bleating, a nanny goat, with full udder. The great nanny goat walked up to Ruth, the oldest woman among them, the great carer, the one who gave love in the love of DOG, who had been so strong in the love of DOG in the concentration camp of the cats. And Ruth took a small clay pot, her only pot, and she milked the great goat. And she gave the milk to a child, who was happy. And the child returned the pot, and Ruth pulled on the teats of the great nanny goat again, and filled the pot and gave it to another child. And again she milked the great nanny goat, yet the udder remained full, milking and milking. After the children had drunk of the sweet milk, the humans each tasted the milk of the goat and they were satisfied. But the dogs could not drink the milk, it made them sick. Then the giant nanny goat, bigger than any human, lay down, and she gave birth to a kid. And then to another kid, and then another kid was born, and another and another so that there would be meat for every dog. And the humans drank of the milk, and the dogs ate of the kids, all sharing, all giving.

Then the great nanny goat got up and bleated. She bleated long and long. And they knew that she was hungry. So the humans gathered the wheat and barley and they gave her the fodder. She ate and ate, all the night she ate. And in the morning her udder was full, and in the evening she gave birth to many kids. And the sun shone strong and warm, and the water in the stream flowed clear, and they grew strong again. They grew strong on the milk and the meat together. Day after day they ate and praised DOG, and in the sun they dried meat from the kids for the day when they would continue their journey.

Then on the 66th day, in the clearing there came a bark, a whisper of a bark. So low, so soft, coming from the sky, from the earth, from the North, from the South, from the East, from the West, and coming from within each dog, from within each human. Louder it came, and louder but sweet, insistent to make them alert, yet friendly as a lick. And each realized that this was the Bark of DOG. And within them, within each man, within each woman, within each bitch, within each dog, within each child, within each puppy, they knew that this was the bark of DOG.

And DOG barked unto each of them, that they heard within them and without them:

> I love thee and will love thee forever.
> Keep thou my covenant:
> - Be kind.
> - Be generous.
> - Count not the giving and the taking, but give unconditionally.
> - Harm no human.
> - Harm no dog.
> - Keep from thee hate, greed, vengeance, lust, fear, gluttony, pride, impatience, indifference, sloth, schadenfreude, guilt, and allergy, for these are the way of CAT.
> - Put from thee all thought of power save the power of a loving heart.
>
> Remember that I am the Lord thy DOG. Walk always with my breath in your ear, my paw upon your heart, my scent ahead leading you on.

Keep thou my covenant, and though you may die, you will live forever, live in the flow, the great flow of love that gathers us all.

I will love thee forever, for you are mine, as I am yours, and we are all together.

ARF

And each man, each woman, each bitch, each dog, each child, each puppy heard, and understood. And they knew they would grow strong in the love of DOG, a love that leads them to give, a love that leads them to be loving. And they celebrated this great Bark of DOG, the Arf of the Covenant.

They built a fire, and they roasted the meat with the fat dripping, and they celebrated, the sun warm upon their backs. Then they danced, they danced in a circle, each dog taking gently in his teeth the tail of the one in front, each human taking the hand of the one in front extending the other hand behind in a great circle, they twirled, they sang, they barked, they yipped, for there was joy again, the joy of the love that NAV has brought from DOG. They would be saved to carry the love of DOG first to the promised land, and then to all the world, to all who had ears to hear, who had eyes to see, who had noses to smell.

And they would remember, they would commemorate each year what they had lived in the forest of rain, the Arf of the Covenant, holding dear to them the memory of the Fodder, the Sun, and the Holy Goat.

The Bringer of Drink

She was young, a human misshapen, her back hunched, walking slowly as she dragged her lame foot. She would not look directly at others. All men and all women shunned her, fearing the hunched back as a sign. There she survived in the craggy mountains North of the great Middle Sea, in the cold forest of the winter and the hot summers of the valley.

Then one night Juninho, a black and white puppy in a great line from Juney, came to her, Juninho, fearful and cold, abandoned, and she cared for him. She cared for him and in caring for him learned to care for others, learned to let her lovely yellow hair flow out, her face round with a great smile of joy and love. She learned to walk lightly in the love that Juninho gave her to give to all others. She learned to look at others, for there was no shame, no fear in the love of DOG.

One night, deep in the night, when the sky was black and sprinkled with many stars, she, the young misshapen one, heard a bark, a great bark, so great the trees shook, a bark that came from nowhere and everywhere. And she was afraid. Juninho jumped up, he ran in a circle, he howled, he came to her and led her out of her hut, led her to the sky, and they heard together the great bark. And together they knew this was the Bark of DOG, a bark for them. But she knew not what it meant. Then Juninho, in yips and yelps and barks and whimpers explained to her that they must go, that they had a great mission. She could not understand, but Juninho pushed her to gather her rags, her broken knife, and to gather especially seeds of the plants they grew for food to put into a small bundle. She was puzzled. But she gathered her rags, her broken knife, the seeds of the plants they grew for food, and waited for the dawn. Then they set out.

In yips and yelps and barks and whimpers, slowly over many days, as they journeyed ever to the West, she learned of the great mission DOG had given her to fulfill with Juninho. To Juninho He had given the knowledge of how to make drinks that would help humans see Him. Juninho knew that NAV would guide them, that NAV would help them, and that NAV would let him teach this knowledge to her, to she who could speak, so she could teach the humans.

They travelled North to the land of the barbarians, of the humans whose speech sounded like growling, near the Danube. They saw them there, with dogs at their side, yet unsure of the love that DOG could give them, unsure of the love that they could give to all. Juninho and she who was misshapen met them, and the humans accepted them because they so admired Juninho, yet they feared the stigma of the hunchback. And the dogs accepted them with joy for they could smell upon them the mission of DOG, though they knew not what it was nor how it would be fulfilled.

The Bringer of Drink

It was Spring, and there in the black forest of the center of the land, near the Danube, they took out some of the seeds that she who was misshapen had carried with them. And they planted the seeds. Then slowly, in the perfect Spring and Summer, the seeds sprouted and grew, and from the few seeds a field, a valley, two valleys were covered in barley, green, like waves in the wind. Then Summer was ending, the nights came early, the barley ripened into gold, and she taught the humans to gather the seed, sharp though the bristles were, and collect the seeds in bags, in wooden tubs, in anything they could carry. She taught them to set aside some, a bag, then another bag, and another bag for next year. Thus they learned how to turn the earth, to sow, and to harvest. She taught them to mill the barley. Much they kept for cakes they burned on the fire. But some, she showed, was to be mixed with water and heated. This they did in the clay pots they had, they followed her, for Juninho would not let them stray, Juninho would gather them, and they would watch. They boiled the barley, and Juninho went out, barking, running, and with the children collected from vines in the valley small fruits of the vines, the hops, and they brought the hops in a bag to she who was misshapen, who put them into the boiling water of barley. Then they let the boiled water and barley cool. They left it, and Juninho would let none approach the pot. They let it cool one day. Then another, and it began to froth. And another, and the froth continued to grow, light upon the brew. Until on the sixth day Juninho barked. And she who was misshapen came to the pot and poured the foaming liquid malt into jars. Then she drank of the liquid, and Juninho barked a great bark and they knew that they should call this "beer." And she offered it to each of the humans. And the humans drank, the six elders, men and women whom all would trust, they drank, first one, then another. Then the younger ones, but not the children, Juninho would not allow them to drink. The children must grow, must learn before they could drink to see Him whose Bark was all. Nor would she let the dogs drink, Juninho growling and nipping, for the dogs had no need of it, they could already see DOG clearly if they would open their hearts. When all the men and women had drunk and found that the taste was good, they sensed a small buzzing in their heads. And she who was misshapen led them to the second pot, and they drank of the liquid again, and they were happy, and they laughed. And the love they had for one another became greater, and they would drink more of this beer. But Juninho would not let them. They must drink only this much, no more, for with this they were open, with this they were able better to see the love of DOG.

She and Juninho had led some men and women to brew the beer to see DOG better, and had taught them so they could teach others to grow the barley, to collect the hops, to brew the beer. And Juninho had taught the dogs of the love of DOG that they could smell in every scent in the wind. She rested then with them, and she was glad. The humans, too, were glad for the gift of beer, glad to give gifts to them, gifts of skins to keep warm and meat to eat. But the men and women did not accept the misshapen one. Though filled with greater love than before, they could not accept she who was misshapen, fearing it a curse. So in the dark of Winter, in the cold and snow, she and Juninho set off for the West. NAV would guide their steps, for they knew that their mission was not ended. As she left the men and women near the Danube, she taught them to say farewell in the love of DOG, so that now at parting they say "Arfwiedersehen."

They traveled during the day, covered in the skins of sheep that the humans had given them. They traveled West, always West, following the scent that NAV gave them, until they reached the river of the small horses, the Roan. They met there a dog unlike any they had ever seen, not big, not small, but powerful and friendly, she with curly hair and prancing walk, and smart, she who was called Fifi. Fifi smelled Juninho and knew that Juninho and the misshapen one were on a mission from DOG, and she barked with joy. Juninho smelled Fifi and knew that Fifi was on a mission from DOG, and he barked with joy. But Juninho was sad for Fifi, for she had not yet found the human who would walk with her, who would collect the vines, to teach others how to grow the vines, how to take the grapes from the vines to make a liquid that would bring the humans closer to the vision of DOG. Then the misshapen one stroked Fifi, poor Fifi who had no human. And Fifi was glad and knew that some day she, too, would have a human to love, but now must continue her mission. So she continued south, and as she went Juninho barked to her to have hope, "Bone chance." And Fifi barked back, knowing of the sea they must come to, "Bone voyage."

The misshapen one and Juninho came then to the great sea, the cold, dark sea. There they found a human at the shore, an old woman seated on the rocks with a small boat, a woman who fished in the sea. The misshapen one came to her. But the woman would not acknowledge her. Then Juninho came to the woman and placed his head in her lap as she sat sorting fish. And the old woman was glad. So she took them on her small barque, with small, small sail, the misshapen one and Juninho, onto the cold dark sea, Juninho barking to head North, ever

North, and the old woman glad, for each day she caught more fish and more fish. Until, across the sea Juninho barked that they should land on the great island in the North. He licked the old woman, and the old woman stroked him, and, finally, she gave to the misshapen one a smile, a gift, the only gift she knew how to give.

There in the cold North they found humans who had sheep. And the humans had oats, and they made a fearful meal from the stomach of a sheep and the oats, a meal they called "haggis." Juninho was happy, he taught the dogs there to herd the sheep, barking and turning them. And the humans accepted the misshapen one because they could see a certain clarity of focus, of mission upon her, they could see in her face a determination that was spread with love.

Then it was Spring and the misshapen one took from her bundle the few seeds, and taught the humans to grow barley. And when the barley was ripe, the misshapen one taught them to gather the seeds. Then, as she saw in a vision from NAV, over a fire they roasted the seeds, but the fire was not of wood, for there were few trees. The fire was of earth, the earth that burns, from the earth that was black and moist yet when dry would burn. They roasted the barley and put it into kettles with water and they boiled it, long and long. Juninho looked for the vine of the small fruit of hops, but could find none. And the misshapen one smiled, for she knew that none was needed. They brewed, and the froth came, and they made the malt. And on the fifth day the froth was ever greater, and the humans would drink. But the misshapen would not let them. These humans who had given the gift of their caring, of their acceptance, for them NAV had a greater gift, much greater. From the misshapen one's dream of NAV came the knowledge to make vessels from copper, to shape small tubes, to take the malt they had made and put it into the vessels, sealing them except for the tube, and to build a fire beneath the vessels. Then through the tubes, in curve after curve, came drop by drop a clear liquid, not murky like the brew from the barley, but clear, and smelling strongly. The humans were afraid to drink, but she who was misshapen took a small clay cup, and drank of it. She coughed, for it was strong, like fire in the water, but she was glad. And she gave to the six elders, men and women whom all would trust. Each took a small sip, strong, so strong the drink, like fire in the mouth and throat, yet warming and smiling was the drink. Like fire in the throat, and with the odor and taste of the fire of the burning earth. And they named it "whiskey," and it was good. And they called it the nectar of the dogs.

The dogs, all the companions in love of the humans, they would drink, too. They each whined and whined to taste of this liquid that could help them see more clearly the way of DOG. But the misshapen one, her yellow hair falling over her hunchback, told them that they were not to drink, for DOG had given them his scent already. Said she, "No whiskey. No whine. Drink to me only with thine eyes." And they looked with love to her and to their humans.

Then the humans would drink more. But the misshapen one stopped them, for she knew from her dream that a little was good and a lot was bad. They must be open to the vision of DOG but not dizzy, not falling down as one young man did. They must drink only enough that they may better know the love and power of DOG and with that the love of each other. And they discovered the great truth that NAV had led them to:

> Malt does more than millions can to justify DOG's ways to man.

Now the mission of Juninho and the misshapen one was done. They could rest. Always before, humans had accepted them only for the gifts they gave. But there, in the North land of sheep, they could stay. There with the dogs that Juninho had shown to herd the sheep, there in the land of haggis and whiskey, the men and women had learned to share, and they could remain.

Then to that land came a stranger, yet one who was close in family to those who ate of the haggis and drank of the whiskey. He, too, was short, with a foot turned under, like the knot at the end of a club. But he was of good cheer, happy and open to all, he smiled at the laughter of the small children who would mock him. With the two dogs that accompanied him he went to the children and played with them. And the children laughed and played. He, too, with flowing yellow hair. And she, the misshapen one, saw that he was good, though not comely he had a heart that gave and that gave always more and that he did not brood on his misfortune. And he looked at her and saw great beauty in her love and the touch of DOG. Seeing her smile, her round face, he brought his two black and white dogs to her fire, to her and Juninho, and they sat. And over the fire they talked, and the dogs grew friendly, the two female dogs and Juninho. And he turned to her, after many nights talking and the dogs snuffling and coming close to one another, and he touched her. And she thrilled, and she touched him. And they drew close. And in their love the villagers saw a greatness, a spark of that which they, too, would like to know. And they were accepted, and they had children. And Juninho of the misshapen one and the two dogs of he of the club foot were close and had many puppies.

The Capture of Schadenfreude

The misshapen one, the girl who had brought the gift of drink, of whiskey to the land in the North, the land of haggis and kind people, she was now a woman. Happy in the love of Juninho, the black and white dog who had come so far with her in her mission to bring the gift of drink. Happy in the love of him with the clubfoot who was kind and open and loving. And happy that she could love, that she could give, each day, helping all, remembering the bark of NAV she had learned so long ago:

    Never pass up an opportunity to be generous.

In the long nights of Winter, one of the puppies of Juninho and the smaller of the two dogs that loved him with the clubfoot, a puppy, small, the runt of the litter, she drew close to Juninho, for she wanted to learn of DOG and the way of love. And Juninho taught her what he knew of DOG, of what he had learned long ago from the tablets that had come from the days of Sultan and Boris. He taught her to put all that is catty from her heart, to be wary of FERRATSI, the mountain lion who prowled the earth for CAT, and to be wary always, sniffing, alert for the presence of the twelve cats of CAT, being HATE, GREED, VENGEANCE, LUST, FEAR, GLUTTONY, PRIDE, IMPATIENCE, INDIFFERENCE, SLOTH, SCHADENFREUDE, GUILT, and ALLERGY. She learned, and she told the other dogs, and together they barked to the humans to be wary of CAT.

Then as the days lengthened, as the air became warm and softer, she, the runt of the litter, smelled in the air a fearful odor of cat. An odor, the odor that Juninho had warned her of. And she searched for Juninho, but he was gone with the misshapen ones to herd the sheep. So she went to her brothers and sisters, all bigger, all stronger, corralling them, barking and yipping. For there was great danger, they must search out the horrible presence of CAT.

They ran out to the dales, to the hills, following the small one, the runt of the litter, who knew of the ways of CAT from Juninho. And they saw in the distance a large cat, quite beautiful, silky hair, licking herself, cleaning so she would be admired by all. And the puppy, the runt of the litter, saw that it was SCHADENFREUDE, one of the twelve cats of CAT. A horror, she barked, a horror, and they all chased, one dog and another, barking, yipping, great with the strength of the pack in the hunt. They chased the cat in a line, then one of them jumped out yipping to cut off that direction, each chasing, each turning the cat, bringing SCHADENFREUDE in a circle closer and closer to them all. And they grabbed SCHADENFREUDE, for they were many and they knew of DOG.

The Capture of Schadenfreude   105

Then she who was the runt of the litter knew that this was cause for celebration, to add to the great celebration at the longest day of the year, when there is no night but only a grayness between the sun almost setting and the sun almost rising. They took SCHADENFREUDE, screeching and clawing, held fast in their teeth, to the huts. There they found a bag of leather, and they put SCHADENFREUDE into it. Then when Juninho and the misshapen ones and Juninho's mates returned, they proudly showed the bag, and she who was the runt of the litter and her litter mates all yipped while hitting the bag. And SCHADENFREUDE screeched and screeched and screeched. And the humans were afraid, for the screech was a terrible sound.

Then Juninho barked with great force that they should no longer hit the bag. "Never, never, even with a cat, shall we take joy in the pain of another. That is the way of CAT." And the puppies all stopped, abashed, hanging their heads, their tails between their legs. Looking down, they waited. And Juninho barked with she who was misshapen, his love with the long yellow hair, now streaked with grey. And she, the misshapen one listened and whispered with Juninho. They came to all the others, to the dogs who had captured this horrid cat of CAT, and told them they would wait until morning. Then they would take out of the bag this horrid cat of CAT and kill it, mercifully, ridding the world of SCHADENFREUDE in a great ritual.

Thoughtfully they all went to build a fire to cook their haggis. And a small child, the darling little one of the misshapen ones, only slightly hunched, with her flowing yellow hair, she came curious to the bag. She, Pandora, opened it. And SCHADENFREUDE leapt out, screeching, clawing, and ran, and ran, and ran, so fast that none could catch her, so that today, still, SCHADENFREUDE lives to torment us all. And Pandora cried. And the humans were afraid, some of them angry that the misshapen one did not punish her thoughtless child. But to punish is not to teach, she said, to punish is to hurt, to walk in the way of CAT. No, she took the little one, she took Pandora and comforted her, for Pandora was afraid, she had seen SCHADENFREUDE who had gone into the bag all lovely with silky fur and had come out twisted with great clumps of hair gone, with twisted face. Then Juininho came to Pandora and licked her and lay down by her side, placing his head in her lap. And slowly Pandora calmed, knowing the peace of love that Juninho gave her.

The days became warmer, the days lengthened more, and the shadow of the sun on the great stone paw on the ridge showed that soon would be the longest day of the year, the day with no night. They began to collect wood for a great fire for the long twilight that would not be night, the humans searching far, returning with a log, then another, and the dogs carrying sticks with them. They would celebrate, for the barley, the oats had been planted, the day was long, they would dance and celebrate and thank DOG for a good summer of rain and sun to ripen their fields.

Then one, a tall woman, the only one with black, black hair, flowing around her head and down her back, tall and sure, she was touched with a greatness by DOG. She thought of how SCHADENFREUDE had howled within the leather bag, of the horrible screeching. And she could see a way to make such a sound without hurting any cat, any person, a sound that would remind them of the horrors of CAT yet which would harm no person, no dog, not even a cat. She went to her hut and took the skin of a sheep, a small part, tanned and clean, and made a bag of leather. She covered it with the many-colored cloth woven from the wool that all the humans wore. She attached pipes to it, carved in them small holes, and carefully placed in each pipe a small reed. Then she took the sap from a tree, a tree from far away, and sealed the bag so air could enter only in the one big pipe with no holes and could go out only through the small pipes. And she tried it, and she could make a sound. But she knew not how to make a melody.

So she took it to Pandora, the little one, still burdened with anxiety and guilt from the sight of SCHADENFREUDE clawing and fleeing free. The tall one, she with the black, black hair, gave the bag with pipes to Pandora and showed her how to blow into the bag and how to put her fingers over the holes in the pipes. And Pandora blew, and behold, she could make a sound, and she was happy. And she blew again, and the light of DOG descended on her and she made a melody. A simple melody, then more, using all the pipes, and the tall one, she with the black, black hair, danced, her hair twirling with her, delighted, and the men and the women came, and the dogs, all curious and then filled with joy. Pandora, said the tall one with the black, black hair, had brought them the gift of music. Pandora alone had the gift of DOG, and she, the tall one with black, black hair had done only what DOG had shown to her.

Then the fire was lit, the longest day had turned into the twilight that would last until rosy-fingered dawn would arise in the East. And they danced to the sound of the pipes, of the melody that sounded like cats being tortured. And one, a big, husky, strong man, known only for his work, his hard work planting and reaping, he with little words, with no-color hair, with eyes that were pink, he sang, yes, for the first time there was song, words that lilted on the melody:

> Should arf acquaintance be forgot and never brought to mind?
> We'll drink a cup of kindness dear, for days of arf lang syne.

Then all joined, looking one to another, the dogs howling, too, and they knew love. And the tall woman, beautiful beyond all others, with black, black hair, went to him with no color, took him by the hand and danced. And he, unsure, listening to the music, singing, putting one foot, then another in the melody and rhythm that Pandora played, he danced. And the day that had no end, the twilight until the dawn, was joyous.

Then Pandora was revered, no longer looked at with fear. And he of no-color was honored for the words he could bring to the music. And the tall one with black, black hair and the strong no-color one were joined forever in love from that longest day, that day with no night. And DOG saw that it was good.

In the Village of
Sadhu-Shwa

Dusk. The soft warm air, with many scents of hay and flowers, trees and rich black earth. The men, the women returning from the fields near the Ganges, the fertile land close to the Ganges. Returning there, close to the forests of the big cats and large elephants where long ago Feral had kept guard. Feral, of the twelve disciples of NAV, DOG's only Puppy, Feral, the wild one, unkempt, with head too big and paws too small, always alert, always scenting for danger. Feral who lived what all dogs now remember:

> Bark first. Ask questions later.

The men and women returning, each with one dog or two scenting ahead, careful. Some come with their tools, others swinging their arms, free at last from pushing the plow that the great ox Bella pulled. The women strong and laughing, the girls laughing more, for these are people who follow the tradition of Ralph, the first of the followers of NAV, with his purple coat, his look aslant and always joking, always wry and teaching through his jabs, through the laughter. The men and women happy to return to the children there at the gathering place under the great bodhi tree.

They come to the fountain and washed, a woman, a man, a dog lapping the clear water, one, another, refreshed. They come to where the men had prepared the meal, the broth of grains and greens. Tonight there is luck, for the dogs have caught two rabbits, rabbits that had been eating in the garden, so there is meat in the broth and the dogs will have bones and a little meat. Not hurrying, one then another they come to the kettle to take their share of broth. There the cripple sits, he whose legs cannot move, he serves the broth into the bowls, happy that he can help, near him his faithful friend, his great companion, Hixny, the terrier who will not stay still, who brings the cripple whatever he calls for, happy to serve him, and he happy to serve her. First they bring the small one who is like a child, with head too big, always smiling, able to understand only a little, drooling, but loving more than any, head aslant, happy, the very spirit of love and the joy of Ralph, they serve him first, making sure he eats. Never does he cry, for always what is is the way of DOG for him in his love.

Then the others, the children first, then the men and women. Each takes a little, leaving more for the others, all sharing, for they had long ago driven out the horrid cat called GLUTTONY. Where there is love in their hearts, where there is sharing and trust, there is no room for GLUTTONY nor GREED nor LUST not even FEAR, the most terrible of the cats of CAT. They sit, one, then another, all calm, talking a little, happy to be with each other, settling themselves, beginning to eat.

Then racing into the clearing, racing comes Tall, the biggest of them, a man so big, so tall. Racing, panting, he cries "Maya, Moya dead." Maya, the light one, thin and comely, she with long hair and a happy smile for all, and Moya, the small black dog, always playful. All start up. They drop their bowls, the dogs run with them, there to the field at the fork in the road, close to the forest edge Tall shows them. "I was there. Next field. Lulu, too. Lulu no barking. I hear nothing. Then terrible barking—Moya. Barking. Too late. Tiger. Big orange and black tiger, white belly. Pounced. Swatted. Moya fought. Biting, biting. Maya saw. Ahead of me, she ran. To Moya. She had her knife. She cried, 'Moya, I come. Do not give up. I come.' The tiger looked. The tiger bites Moya. The tiger she leaps at Maya. The tiger leaped. The tiger swatted Maya. Awwwwful. Her face, the huge paw, sharp claws. Awwwwful. I run. Lulu ahead, so big, strong, her great bark. The tiger saw, ran. The tiger afraid, the great bark. We so big. Running, I see Maya and Moya. Maya bleeding. Her face crushed. Crawling, crawling to Moya. Moya whimpering, crawling to Maya, her legs crumpled, crawling. Struggling they reached. Maya touched Moya. Moya licked Maya. Maya embraced her big-hearted dog. There, see. Together. Dead. Both dead."

Tall says no more. He is not eloquent. He cannot say what he feels. He can only describe. None is so eloquent. They cannot say what is in their hearts, they know not what it is. They are sad. Yet all are happy, too, for here is the greatest way to die, to die in love, to die embracing your beloved, unafraid, dog and human close to the very end.

Then Gaia, the old strong woman, with full thick black hair only now beginning to gray, Gaia, upright and strong, tells a young boy to fetch a shovel, and even before the shovel comes they begin to dig a grave there for Maya and Moya. The humans with their hands, the dogs with their feet dig the dark rich earth. And when the shovel arrives, Tall begins to dig, tears in his eyes, digging a deep hole, a deep hole, so deep no tiger will disturb the last of Maya and Moya. They place the bodies there in the deep deep hole. They cover them, filling the hole with the black earth. And a dog begins to howl, not sorrow but loneliness, and another dog, and the humans howl, too, until it becomes a song, their song of remembrance:

No man is an island (the men sing)
No dog is an island (the dogs howl)
No woman is an island (the women sing)
No man stands alone (the men sing)
No dog stands alone (the dogs howl)
No woman stands alone (the women sing)
Each man's joy, each dog's joy, each woman's joy is joy to me.
Each man's grief, each dog's grief, each woman's grief is my own.

They mourn for their loss, but they have joy in the great example of Maya and Moya.

Then Gaia says, "Let us rejoice that they have gone into the great flow of all, the flow of love, the flow of love of DOG. Gone they are but still here, their substance changed but their form and love continue." And as they sing, Gaia goes with the shovel to a small bodhi sapling. She digs it up, carefully, and carries it to the resting place of Maya and Moya. There she plants it. And they dance, small steps, on the fresh-turned earth, packing down the earth as they dance, packing down with their dance so no tiger will disturb and the tree will grow strong. Then a small boy runs off and returns with water, and first Gaia, then another pours water on the tree, the boy running off for more, until each has poured a little water on the earth that the tree should grow strong as the love of those beneath it. Then each dog goes to the tree and makes a single drop of water on the earth, a scent to remember that they have loved Maya and Moya. A loss, but a great time of joy of the death in love that is greater than death.

Then all return, slowly, to the gathering place. They eat quietly, murmuring. Death has come, but love is stronger than death. And they begin to talk. The children who stayed behind begin to run, to chase, and the little dogs follow them, nipping at their heels, and the men and women smile. Life continues: these young ones shall learn to love. And they begin to talk.

Dulix, an old man, who lives in the way of Ralph, always joking, always wry and teaching through his jabs, through the laughter, Dulix who helps them follow the way of love through laughter, asks, "How many cats does it take to knit a sweater?" And a little boy pipes up, knowing the response, "I don't know. How many?" And Dulix says, "One. It just sits on your lap and won't let you get up until you finish it for her." And they smile a little. Then Dulix asks, "How many cats does it take to feed a family of four?" And the little boy begins to say again, "I don't . . ." when all hush him, laughing lightly. Then Dulix asks,

"How many cats does it take to bring true love to your heart?" And an old woman whispers to the boy that he can ask now, and the boy says, "I don't know. How many?" And Dulix responds, "No one knows yet."

They relax a little, glad to be together, knowing, as followers of Ralph, that a joke can lead the way from sorrow to the truth of love. Then a young man, handsome and dark, strong, says, "Gaia, you are wise." And Gaia smiles, "Not wise. Only a good memory for the Bark of DOG." And he continues, "Tell us, how can it be? In the next village, you know, there is a woman who sings, she sings so beautifully, Vishna she is called, so beautifully. Yet she has a cat, no, two cats, and she worships there in the village at the temple of CAT. She sings so beautifully, though all know she steals the songs from others, she is filled with hate for her rivals, she pets her cats and smiles as they torture mice or little birds. How can it be that she sings so beautifully when there is no love in her heart?"

And Gaia replies, "Oh, there is love in her heart, but only love for herself. That is how she follows the way of CAT. Men want her, I hear, they want her, and she lets them make love to her. But hers is an ersatz love, taking and taking and taking but never giving. It is the love and way of CAT that is no love."

And the young man asks again, "But how can she sing so beautifully? We all cry when we hear her, we are moved, yet she has no real love in her heart. How can a follower of CAT make such beauty?"

Then Gaia reflects. "There is a bark, an ancient bark from Akita, the Third DOGGY LAMA:

    All who are sentient have the capacity to love.
    All who are sentient are here with the chance to love.

So this seed of love is in her, and it comes out in her singing. She is moved to love though she cannot recognize it in herself. She preens herself as a cat, but inside her is the capacity to love that shines forth in her songs, unknown to her. We cannot abandon her, we cannot hate her."

"No," says another young cripple, with his dog so close to him, a young man bringing him a bowl with the broth. "No, it is not her love that is in the singing, for she has no love of anyone nor any thing but herself. No, she sings beautifully to be admired, and we, who can love, we who do have the spark of love within us, growing, always growing, . . ." and many people murmur, "May it be DOG's will," and many dogs yip a little, ". . . it is our love that responds to the beauty in her song. She just plucks the string; it is we who reverberate. You are right, we must not hate her, for that is the way of CAT. Nor, surely, should we admire her, nor be envious of her wealth and power. Yes, there is a temple of CAT in that village. Yes, the village there is rich. The riches they take from others. In land and gold it is rich, in much power. But it is a false power, the power to hurt, to hold on to what they have because of the fear lest it be taken."

"Yes," says Gaia, "the fear is masked as power. They are not rich. We are rich, rich in love. We care for all, the strongest and the weakest. We share our food so none go hungry or all go hungry. We have our small portion of land. We need no more. And they do not try to take it from us. They have learned that though we will not fight them—for we will harm no human, harm no dog—we will die for our love of each other if they attack. And though they be followers of CAT, the little love they have in them responds when we sit in the road, when we touch each other and sing as they come towards us with evil. They will not harm us because they are ashamed. We try to teach them that in harming us they harm themselves. So they leave us alone. And rarely, sometimes, a man or a woman, perhaps old, perhaps young, perhaps strong, perhaps weak, comes to our village to learn of love." And some look at Grzzk, a man almost old, a little bent, who has come from the village of the followers of CAT not so long ago, who has sought help to learn the light of love. And they smile, and Grzzk nods, yet unsure to talk, but he nods, and smiles, stronger now in the love he has found he can give.

Then a young girl says, "But in the village there is a man, WeeB, who is good. He is rich, and he gives much gold to feed the poor every week."

"Good!?" "Good!?" says Gaia. "He is rich. He turns the sweat of the poor into gold, "his" gold. They work and work and work, yet they earn so little they cannot feed themselves. He starves them, then feeds them a little from the gold they have brought him. I have seen him. He is attended always by the ugly cats PRIDE and GREED—he calls them his servants, but it is he who is their servant. He is proud that he can give to the poor; he wants all to admire him. Yet he keeps much, almost all the gold and land and harvest to satisfy GREED. Remember the bark of Buddy, the 16th DOGGY LAMA:

> It is easier for a camel to pass through the eye of a needle
> than for a rich man to have a loving heart.

And the bark of Lorilar, the 17th DOGGY LAMA, who learned from Buddy:

DOG loves an open hand and a closed mouth."

The one with head too big, drooling, always smiling, able to understand only a little, he smiles, he coos, and they look to him, each petting him a little, and they are all happy. For they love, they share. They live in the words of Hezekibah, the Forty-Ninth DOGGY LAMA:

From each according to his ability, to each according to his need.

They are content. They have seen great love this day. They have shared. They have eaten together, the young and the old, the strong and the weak, the cripple and the healthy, the wise and the ones who can never understand, the humans and dogs, they are together. They have seen great love, and they give great love.

Morton & Fletch Are Chosen

Dusk. The soft warm air, with many scents of hay and flowers, trees and rich black earth. Along the path comes Morton leading Bella the ox. Morton, not tall, not short, slight, an ordinary man, just past his youth. At his side is Fletch, the faithful one, alert, sniffing the air, running ahead and returning, always alert as was Feral, the great disciple of NAV, who long ago roamed here, always alert for the scent of CAT. "Bark first, ask questions later," thinks Fletch, ready always. Fletch, his head too big, his paws too small, some say the very image of Feral so long ago.

They put Bella in the pasture near the gathering place. Tired, a hard day of plowing the rich earth, Morton and Fletch turn to the cleared area under the bodhi tree. Others have come first, some men making the fire, children gathering wood, women and men cooking the broth. All tired. All content to be with the others, women and men and dogs, children and puppies, to share. Maybe tonight, thinks Morton, there will be meat, a rabbit. Or perhaps the young woman Zelda and the young dog Rilly have caught a fox, they are learning quickly. A little to eat, and better a chance to talk, to sit together, all, telling of the day, remembering the days before.

Morton and Fletch walking to the gathering place meet Zelda and Rilly. Beautiful, thinks Morton, she is beautiful and kind, and Fletch loves the scent of Rilly. But though Fletch nuzzles Rilly, Morton says nothing. Shy, saying little, that is his way. No longer young, but not old. Strong enough, but no hero, no great worker, he does what he can. He walks next to Zelda, silent, admiring. And she, shy but talking much, she is glad. They walk together, with Fletch and Rilly trotting side by side.

They come with their bowls to the great bronze kettle, they take the broth of grains and greens. No meat tonight. But they are content. All are content to talk, humming and murmuring, sharing, telling of the long day in the sweet, moist warm air. Morton silent, listening, intent to listen when the stories are told of the disciples of NAV, DOG's only Puppy whom DOG sent to teach of love. These he loves, the disciples in the stories, the great ones. He glances shyly at Zelda, and she smiles a great smile to him. She knows that Morton is for her, Morton, so shy, not strong, not a hero, but strong in the way of love, strong in his heart for the good way of peace. She knows she is for him. And she is glad.

Darkness, the flickering light of the fire, all tired. Morton gets up, Fletch quickly at his side. He nods at Zelda, Fletch nuzzles at Rilly, Zelda smiles a great smile, then Morton and Fletch go to their hut. Morton washes his hands, washes his face with the water in the bowl. Fletch laps a little, Morton stroking him. Then Morton kneels before his pallet, saying as he says each night before sleep, "Our Father who arf in heaven, howled be thy name. Thy kingdom come, thy will be done, with arf as it is in heaven." He says this for comfort, an old prayer, though he knows there is no heaven, even he, so simple knows that heaven is here, giving with a loving heart. There is no hell, he knows, they all know, only the hell of knowing you could have helped but didn't. Heaven he would live each day; hell he would try to avoid each day. He prays only because the words sound good, a sound to remind him of the great flow of all, no kingdom but the flow of love. Then he says the prayer that is no prayer but a reminder for all, "Guide me to have a loving heart." He thinks of Zelda and curls up on his pallet. He reaches out to Fletch, curled up against his back. He sleeps.

And in the night he feels a breath in his ear, a lick at his ear. He touches his ear, he feels for Fletch, touching him, still curled at his back lying quietly. Odd. Then the breath again, the little lick. He turns, he sits up. Fletch whines and wags his tail. There is a presence, a sweet smell. And Morton hears—though there is no sound—the bark of DOG, "Among the many, you are chosen." And Fletch, lying with his paws in front, gazing up, not at Morton, twitches his nose at the sweet smell, a smell he knows is stronger than the smell of death. And Fletch hears, too, the bark of DOG. They are chosen.

They know then they have a mission, to spread the bark of DOG, this they know. There, on his arm, in the nearly light of dawn, Morton sees the Mark of DOG, the place where DOG has touched him, a paw print black on his arm. He and Fletch are chosen to teach, to give the bark of DOG to those who know not the way of love and peace, to carry the wisdom of love that he has been learning at the fire each night, to carry the wisdom of love to those who know not yet how to love. Then Fletch licks Morton's face, near his mouth, licking again, for Fletch knows they are chosen. They are only ordinary, and Morton so shy, so hard for him to talk, Morton and Fletch must go forth to teach the way of DOG, the way of love and peace. Morton holds Fletch's head in his hands, they look deeply into each other's eyes, and Morton says, "In the middle of the path of our life, we have a new road. A new way we must go. We were not lost, but now we are found."

Together they will go forth, to show love in their bearing, they will give love in their actions, and they will teach the few words that Morton has. Morton will learn to talk and to sing of the love of DOG, and Fletch, alert, will learn to make small barks to the dogs he will meet. Together. Always. They will go.

That day Morton goes to the fields with Fletch, the fields he has plowed with Bella the ox, the fields he will not now sow nor reap. Bella in the next field, an old man helped by others to guide the plow she pulls. Fletch is alert, quiet, ready, sniffing the air for their mission. Morton thinks, and he knows that he must leave the village of Sadhu-Shwa, to leave all they have known, the great love of all, the giving and taking, the sharing, the place where his mother and father are buried, where Maya and Moya are buried, though they are always with him in the great flow of love that surrounds all and is all. They will leave all they have known, all except the words and barks of the stories and wisdom of DOG and of NAV, DOG's only Puppy, and the twelve disciples of DOG, and the stories of warning of CAT, who would lead through FERRATSI her great mountain lion to the ways of her twelve cats, HATE, GREED, VENGEANCE, LUST, FEAR, GLUTTONY, PRIDE, IMPATIENCE, INDIFFERENCE, SLOTH, SCHADENFREUDE, GUILT, and ALLERGY. Only the wisdom and stories will they carry. They will go out with nothing, only a begging bowl will Morton carry.

He will leave Zelda, Fletch will leave Rilly, though their hearts are full for them. This is the sacrifice, he knows, the suffering through which we learn to love, for without suffering there is no real knowledge of love, no love so deep it can be trusted. They will leave, they will teach, and, DOG willing, they will return to add to the stories at the fire in the clearing under the great bodhi tree.

That night, at the gathering, Morton holds back. He is the last to take a bowl of broth, more shy than ever, almost ashamed that he, so weak and shy, has been chosen. Chosen, DOG said, because of his loving heart. Then as he takes his bowl of broth, as Fletch is given a small bone, the cripple, the one who serves all with great joy, exclaims, "There on Morton's arm, the Mark of DOG, the paw print." The humans look, they come up and touch his arm—the paw print was not there yesterday. The dogs come to him and smell, then making happy barks they go to Fletch and sniff him all over and find a lingering sweet smell. The humans and the dogs exclaim, clapping and yipping, that Morton has the Mark of DOG upon him. Morton, no one would have thought. Shy, quiet, with Fletch, now given the sign of DOG, of DOG's special choice.

Then Morton tells them, haltingly, in a very small voice, so shy, looking down, that DOG spoke to him in small barks that he is chosen to teach, to give the bark of DOG to those who know not the way of love and peace, to carry the wisdom of love he has been learning at the fire each night to those who know not yet how to love. Looking down, so shy, so unsure, such a great mission for such a man as he. Why? He knows not. He has not done anything. But DOG has chosen him. He will leave, journey far from here to teach those who do not know how to love. Not to the next village, the village of CAT, for that is close and all here can help teach those who are lost there in the quest for power. He must travel, and he knows it will be far. He will learn to talk, he will learn to be more than he has been, for love is not love that knows no sacrifice.

They all come to Morton. They kiss his hand, the dogs lick Fletch. Morton is so shy, he looks down, he is nothing special, he thinks, he will do all he can, but he deserves no special kindness nor touch. The last to come to him, to come to Fletch, are Zelda and Rilly. She takes his hand, she kisses it, and Rilly licks Fletch again and again on his mouth. "Return," Zelda says, "with new wisdom to share with us. I shall wait." And Rilly nuzzles up to Fletch before going to the side of Zelda as she, tears flowing hard but with a great smile, walks away. And Morton feels his face burn, he knows that he must carry this love in him to all.

And then, not even waiting for the new dawn, in the dusk, in the twilight, Morton walks down the path, the new path of his life, Fletch at his side, not waiting for the dawn, not looking back, strong yet sad, feeling he must learn to give the power of love to all.

The Journey of Morton & Fletch

Morton, so shy, so quiet, slight, no hero, walks West from his village of Sadhu-Shwa, from his village near the Ganges where the men and women and children live whom he loves so deeply. He walks West, going each day farther, farther from the life he knew. He was chosen by DOG, the giver of peace and the way of love, the way of love that DOG's only Puppy taught them to follow. He was chosen to give the Bark of DOG to those who know not the way of love and peace, to carry the wisdom of love to those who know not yet how to love. So he must leave behind those whom he carries in his heart, whom he feels around him always in the great flow of love.

At his side walks Fletch, the faithful one, alert, sniffing the air, running ahead and returning, always alert, his head too big, his paws too small, some say the very image of Feral so long ago. Fletch chosen, too, to guard, to find those who follow the way of CAT, the ways of HATE and FEAR and PRIDE and GREED and VENGEANCE and LUST and GLUTTONY and IMPATIENCE and INDIFFERENCE and SLOTH and SCHADENFREUDE and GUILT and ALLERGY, the twelve cats of CAT. Alert especially for FERRATSI, the great mountain lion who answers only to CAT, doing her bidding, wanting always to rid the world of the way of DOG, the way of love.

They walk, Morton carrying only his bowl which sometimes a stranger will fill, sometimes a woman will give a bone to Fletch, sometimes, Morton saying, "Since we have left our home, we have always depended on the kindness of strangers." Sometimes Morton takes only a guava, a low-hanging fruit from a tree at the road, Fletch running to catch a mouse or lizard. They eat little, they need little, traveling always West, then a little North, for Morton knows that this must be the way, and Fletch trusts so deeply his human. Sometimes they come to a village, far from the way of DOG, not bad but not yet knowing the way of peace and love. Then Morton tries to teach, he goes to the gathering place, he tries to talk. Stammering, he speaks of DOG's way, of NAV, DOG's only Puppy, of Juney who was the First DOGGY LAMA, he tries. He speaks so softly, so timid, few listen, they pass him by, some putting a crust of bread in his bowl or a little curry, some stopping to pet Fletch. This is all he can do. He must learn, he must learn to talk. He is not eloquent. He has not the words. West and North they walk along the dusty roads, this the new path they had been chosen for in the midst of the path of their life.

North and West. Until they come to the water, the great sea, waves rolling on, waves rolling free. So much water that the Ganges seems small, water for as far as they can see. Fletch, bewildered, curious, goes to the edge of the waves, the wet-packed sand, sniffing, and a wave comes, pushing him down, dragging him out to sea, Morton running after, in the water, grabbing Fletch, pulling, they reach the sand again, panting, exhausted. Fletch rises, shaking himself, licking Morton on the mouth. Licking him. Morton clutching him to his chest, stroking Fletch again and again. The sea is not our friend, they think. They walk along the sea. Morton knows his path must lead West, but he cannot cross this sea. There is no path. They walk along the beach, careful of the waves, beneath the palms, among the sharp grass, stopping to drink from a clear stream that flows into the sea, flows as must their love flow to the great world—so dangerous —of those who know not yet how to love.

They come to a hut. A small hut made of branches from the palms. A little fire in front. And an old woman at the fire, an old woman cooking a fish, so old, her long hair white, but she is strong, her muscles clear upon her arms. They come to her. She sees the Mark of DOG upon Morton's arm and she bows to him, she bows and asks for his blessing. Morton shakes, he shakes and trembles. His blessing? He is nothing, only a poor slight man who was told to carry the Bark of DOG to those who know not. He has no wisdom except—Zelda said now long ago—the wisdom of a loving heart. He kneels and bows to the old woman. He bows. And Fletch comes up, on his belly, he crawls to her and whines. She pets him, she touches Fletch.

Then she speaks. "I see the Mark of DOG upon you. And a sweet smell, so very faint, I scent upon you. You are on a mission from DOG, a mission to teach. This I know. I am here, a woman, with a small boat, only a barque with a single sail. I am here to help. NAV, DOG's only Puppy, has shown me the way of love and peace, and I am here to help. Here, where few, where no one knows of DOG and the way of peace and love. At the edge of the sea I fish each day, I eat, I wait. There is no dog here, none, they have gone, many killed by those who follow CAT. I am alone. But I am not alone, I am in the flow of love, with you. I am here to help."

And Morton and Fletch are glad, they are content, they sit next to her, sharing the fish, the clear water, the little bread and fruit she has. She, she tells them, is called The Old Woman of the Sea. And Morton tells her, so comfortable to be able to speak to one who knows of DOG and of NAV and feels them in her heart, he tells her he knows his path must be West, but he cannot cross this sea.

Then The Old Woman of the Sea starts, abrupt, fearful. "That way," she says, "is a land of cats, of many cats, across the sea, in the heat of the desert across the sea. There is a land of great danger."

"And," Morton says, "of great opportunity. A place to teach. I will find a stronger voice to tell the stories, the wisdom of DOG."

"Then I shall carry you, the two of you, in my small barque. I know the way. It is many days we will be on the sea, eating only the fish we can catch, drinking the little water. By DOG's will we shall arrive. But I cannot stay with you there, no, it is not my mission, mine is to help those who come here. Most go South, to the land of the dark people, to the richer lands, and some return. They call me, I hear, I know not how, and I sail to them, and some return. But some do not. I know not whether they are safe and teaching the way of love and peace or whether they have perished. But to the West I have taken only one, his name Malamud, now many years ago, I put him on the shore and have never heard of him again. No call, no traveler."

Then Morton and Fletch look into each other's eyes. They look, a tear falls from Morton's eye, and Fletch whimpers. They will go. There is no love, no deep knowledge of love if there is no sacrifice and suffering. They will go. Perhaps they will never again see and smell Zelda and Rilly, never again know the sweet scent of the flowers and black rich earth near the Ganges, but they will take the Bark of DOG to those who suffer in the torment of FEAR and HATE and VENGEANCE and LUST and GREED and GLUTTONY and PRIDE and IMPATIENCE and SLOTH and SCHADENFREUDE and GUILT and ALLERGY, the twelve cats of CAT. It is the will of DOG. No—more—it is their will now, to love and to give love and through their sacrifice to learn more deeply of love so they might teach others. "We will go," Morton says, and Fletch barks, wagging his tail, but looking quizzically at the sea. The great sea that they must cross.

They sleep. They rest and eat for three days, talking, Morton learning to talk, for there is no one else to tell the stories and wisdom of DOG. Then on the fourth day the old woman tells them to help her ready her barque, to clean the wood, to caulk with sap from the trees, to stitch the sail. On the seventh day all is ready. Dried fish, a little grain, some dried fruit, and water, as much water as they have pots and skins to carry. Fletch gets into the boat, uneasy, unsure, then Morton and The Old Woman of the Sea push the boat into the water, Morton clambering into it, worried lest a wave take him away, the old woman climbing skillfully into the boat, raising the sail, and they are off. Off across the great sea.

They are on the sea, frightening but exhilarating, the wind, the spray, the rocking of the boat, back and forth, back and forth. And then the nausea, the old woman cheerful, while Fletch whines and Morton turns green. This is suffering, while the old woman sings the songs of the sea, heading always West.

They sail. The Old Woman of the Sea catches fish, she calls to them, she trills, the fish come, some jumping into the boat in ecstasy, to offer themselves to those in the way of DOG. She eats, she tells Morton to eat, and on the third day he begins to eat, now used to the rocking, the swell of the sea, and he coaxes Fletch to eat, a little, then a little more. They survive, The Old Woman of the Sea always cheerful. They will cross the great sea.

On the eighth day they see land, dunes, sand above a beach, palm trees, yes and the smell of sand, of dry earth. Fletch sniffs and barks, at last land, an end of the rocking, the sun and the sea. Morton smiles. And The Old Woman of the Sea frowns, she knows. "It is a dangerous land there," she says. "A few at the village at the beach may help us, give us water for the fish I have caught. Inland, I am told, there is a great city. Expect no kindness there."

They land, the boat running up on the sandy beach, Fletch bounding out, not waiting, bounding then running on the beach, back and forth he runs, yelping with joy. Land again. Morton clambers out, unsteady, helping the old woman drag the boat farther up the beach, tying the boat to a palm. Safe, at last. The earth, though only sand, it is the earth again. He walks, unsteady, Fletch running up to him, back and forth, stretching his legs, while the woman goes to the three men at the edge of the village. They talk, then they return, the men bringing pots of water, she giving them fish, big fish, they smile. For them it is not so easy to catch fish. But she is The Old Woman of the Sea. The men return to their huts, carrying the fish. Then Morton and Fletch come to The Old Woman of the Sea. They bow to her, to her knowledge of the sea and the kindness of her heart. She bows to them. Then Fletch play-bows, and bow wows, and jumps, and there is laughter again, for they had forgotten the way of Ralph, the great disciple of NAV who was always joking, always wry, teaching through his jabs, through the laughter. There is a time to be silly—almost any time, thinks Morton.

"Call me. I will come," says The Old Woman of the Sea. "I wait for your call. May DOG be with you." They part, now happy, now sad, now smiling, now with a tear, they part, Morton and Fletch on the beach, The Old Woman of the Sea sailing farther and farther, Morton waving, Fletch barking. Then Morton and Fletch see a fish, a fish so big leaps from the sea near the barque of The Old Woman of the Sea and slaps the sea with its tail, swimming round, playing, joyful it seems, and they hear The Old Woman of the Sea trilling to it. Then she is gone, beyond where they can see.

Morton & Fletch
in the City of CAT

Morton walks to the gates of the city. A great walled city, with high gates for the carts and horses and camels to pass through, the walls standing heavy in the heat of the desert sun. And Morton thinks, "It is easier for a rich man to pass through the eye of a needle than to be a camel," and he laughs. At last, he can joke, a lightness to ease the burden. Walking in the way of DOG, of NAV, DOG's only Puppy, with his mission from DOG to teach love to those who know not how to love, he can walk, too, in the way of Ralph, the disciple of NAV, always joking, his burden lifted a little. Fletch at his side, Fletch, the faithful one, alert, his head too big, his paws too small, some say the very image of Feral so long ago, Fletch senses the difference, a lightness in the walk of Morton, and he yips. They will teach together, he with his small yips to the dogs, Morton with his stories and the wisdom of DOG, and now with jokes, a little laughter.

They come to the gates of the city. A great image of CAT stands above the entrance, a statue on top of the high wall above the entrance, and written in a scratching script, clear for all to see "Abandon DOG all ye who enter here." This is indeed a city of CAT, a place where the humans have need to learn of love. They pass through, the guards so lazy, so indolent, they do not notice or do not care to stop them. Then Fletch stops, he sniffs, he growls softly, alert, warning Morton. Here, here is cat. He looks at Morton, then stares at the largest guard, a big, fat, sweating man reclining on a couch at the gate, and Morton sees that he has no thumbs, for this is the cat of CAT called SLOTH. SLOTH sees that Fletch is with Morton, that a dog is about to enter the city, but he does not stir. He gazes at them with cat-eyes, malevolent, yet unwilling to get up.

They enter the city. Dusty, sand and stones for the paths between the walls of the houses. Twisting paths continue on and on in a confusing maze. No green, no green at all. Then looking up, Morton sees a palm showing above a wall, some vines along the top of another wall. Inside must be gardens, gardens they hide from all. Truly this is a city of CAT where they do not share the good they have, where FEAR and GREED, the cats of CAT, have power over the men and women.

They continue, Fletch now very close to Morton, Morton with a hand on Fletch, uneasy, the burden of their mission now great. They come to an open area, surrounded by the walls of houses, where a fountain runs, clear water. They go to it. Morton dry with thirst lifts Fletch to drink. A cry from a man, a great cry, "No. Dogs are unclean! No dog may drink from the waters of the fountain."

Unclean? Dogs unclean? Then Morton, still dry with thirst, takes his bowl. He scoops it into the water and walks slowly to a path between walls where none can see, and he puts the bowl down. Fletch laps from it, wagging his tail, looking up at Morton, grateful, wagging, he drinks. Then Morton returns and scoops the bowl into the water again, and again goes with Fletch to the path between the houses where Fletch laps and laps. Then Morton returns to the fountain and drinks with cupped hands, thinking of the ways of DOG, of the mystery that a city can be as great as this and be a land of CAT. A small village like the one near his home on the Ganges could be ruled by those who follow CAT, he knew. But a great city?

Morton sees one man, then another, walking slowly in the heat of the desert sun. Several more, all looking aslant at them, sniffing the air as they pass, the sight of a dog making them uneasy. They see, too, one dog, hurrying, its tail between its legs, thin, scrawny, its bones showing stark against her skin, her dugs dry and low, fearful. Fletch yips softly to her, but she hurries past, fearful, unwilling to stop, and a man throws a stone at her. Terrible. But no man throws a stone at Fletch for he is too close to Morton, and Morton, so slight, not strong, is protection enough.

They come then to a great square, much larger, where there are men selling and buying, many beneath tents, many more with their pots and fruit and bread and cloth and copper bracelets spread on rugs over the sand. Morton goes to a man, dressed lightly, a wide straw hat on his head, he seems rich with gold on his wrist. He is neither selling nor buying, but talking and looking. Others come to him and bow. Morton goes to him and puts his bowl out. The man slaps it away. "Go," he says. "You are a taker. We do not give to those who do not earn their bread." Morton draws back, Fletch at his side, turning, sniffing the air, alert and nervous.

So many men. But where are the women? Then Morton realizes, he sees that those who are covered in black, from the top of their head, no hair showing, to the ground, not even the least part of their feet can be seen, these are the women. Covered in black, in this heat, only a slight opening for their eyes so they do not stumble, and their hands in gloves, black gloves. They do not buy, they do not sell, each walks three paces behind a man. Yes, they are not separate, he now realizes; each follows a man. He cannot understand.

He goes to another man, one with symbols on his white tunic, symbols with pictures of cats. All men who come to him are deferential, bowing, not bowing as to the rich man, but bowing, it seems, in reverence. He has much gold on his hands, around his neck, powerful he must be. A priest, perhaps. Morton goes to him, Fletch behind. "Oh powerful one," Morton says, "I wish to learn the ways of the city here so that I might stay and talk with those who live and love here." The man nods, full of pride, and says, "Ask what you wish. I shall tell you."

Then Morton says, "These who are all in black, whose eyes only can be seen, they are women, are they not?" "Yes," says the priest of CAT, "they wear the fine woven black cloth to cover them. It is called a bearcoat." "A bearcoat?" asks Morton. "Yes. Our ancestors came from the North, the far North, where we are told it is very cold. There they killed the bears and wore their skins, black bears, and the women were covered there, too."

"But why are the women covered?" asks Morton. Then the priest replies, "Lest their skin, their hair, their lips, their hands, their feet excite in us lust. They are covered to remain chaste and so we men will not be tempted."

Then Morton opens his eyes wide, and wider, he stands erect, he seems big, bigger than he has ever been, and he says, "For your lust, not theirs, you make them suffer, you give them no way in the world except the way of a slave? Better that you should pluck your eyes out than to shame and torture women this way for your lust. If thy eye offend thee, pluck it out." He quivers. He has never spoken strongly before, but the voice of DOG is in him.

As Morton speaks, the priest is amused, a beggar, a stranger, admonishing him. But as Morton continues the priest grows angry, and angrier still.

"You must learn to love, to give, to share. Come, take my hand in the path of peace," Morton says, and Fletch comes to his side, whining, looking at the priest, offering himself, too.

Then the priest roars, "Seize them. They do not walk in the way of CAT. They are infidels. Seize them." Many men grab Morton, but Morton will not fight. "Harm no human, harm no dog" is the covenant of DOG. And men circle Fletch, sure that he will bite and scratch, but he will not fight. "Harm no human, harm no dog" is the covenant of DOG. They put a rope around the neck of Morton and pull him, a rope around the neck of Fletch and pull him.

Rough they are, unkind, strong. But Morton will not fight, will not struggle, running, almost dragged along. Worried only for Fletch, he turns, but a fat man slaps him; Fletch yips, and a thin man kicks him. They are pulled, almost dragged to a big square. A great temple is there, columns so high, decorated with many images of CAT, and many cats there, lapping at bowls of milk on the portico. They will not enter, they will not pollute the temple of CAT with an unbeliever and a dog. Morton is held, too far to touch Fletch, but he calls to him, "Fletch. I am with you." And Fletch barks, not yips, and both are struck, Morton with a hand, Fletch with a stick. Morton bleeds a little, but Fletch will not attack. "Harm no human, harm no dog." They will live in the way of love, for their example, their power is no other.

From the interior of the temple a swarthy man comes out, dark, clothed in white, with a big white straw hat shading his face. Four women come behind him, with small steps following, bent forward, eyes on the ground. The priest goes to this man and says, "Oh High Priest! This beggar questions our ways, says we are full of lust, says we should be blinded rather than our women wear bearcoats. And he has a dog, a dog with him! He speaks of love, of peace, but he does not know that women want to wear bearcoats, they are happy to wear bearcoats, it makes them safe, they are safe with us."

The High Priest listens. He looks to be pondering, but he knows already. "He is an infidel. And the dog is unclean." Morton and Fletch wait, they wait, Morton bleeding around the mouth, the side of Fletch swelling where he has been struck. They wait. Will they be let go, allowed to leave the city of CAT? Then a small man comes up to the High Priest. Fletch growls, he barks, and he is struck hard with a stick. Morton looks and sees that the man, in a tunic less ostentatious than that of the High Priest, is more elegant, yet is drooling, rubbing his hands together. And Morton sees that the man has no thumbs, but from his fingers slowly emerge claws, only a little, then retract. Then Morton knows that this is LUST, one of the terrible cats of CAT, servant of FERRATSI, the mountain lion, sent to rid the world of the way of DOG. Morton sees that this is LUST. Morton abandons all hope as LUST whispers in the ear of the High Priest, and Morton says so softly, "Be strong, Fletch, be strong. We walk in the way of love, of peace, of kindness. We shall win their hearts or we shall die, but we shall never harm them, for peace does not grow from violence, love does not grow from violence." He is struck, hard across the mouth. And Fletch barks once, then is struck hard across his muzzle with a stick. He bleeds, but he wags his tail. They are on a great mission from DOG, and if they must suffer, it will be to teach of the way of love, and to learn of the way of love.

Then the High Priest says, "Seize them. Take them there, to the center, for they shall be stoned. It is the will of CAT."

They take Morton to the center of the great square, a round area of dust and sand in the center, and they dig a hole, slowly, while Morton sweats in the sun. And they put him in the hole, up to his neck they put him, and fill the hole with sand. Only his neck and head are above the sand, only his eyes can see, his ears can hear, his nose can smell. And next to him they drive a stake into the ground, a strong metal stake, and they tie Fletch to it, they tie him around the neck. He can move, but he cannot flee. But he would not flee, they need not tie him, for he would never leave Morton, he would not go. He crawls to Morton, but he cannot reach him. Morton turns to Fletch, he smiles, "A great mission my love, a great mission." And Fletch whines, licking, his tongue so close to Morton.

Then three men come carrying a great basket filled with stones. And another three come with a great basket of stones. And another three come with more stones still. Trumpets sound, loud, brackish, and many men come to the square, many men. Then the High Priest says, "Bring the women forward. Bring them forward." And many women are brought forward, all in their bearcoats, all black. "This man says that we should put out our eyes rather than you wear bearcoats. What say you?"

And the women know not what to say. They rejoice to hear that a man could see their sorrow. They rejoice but they are afraid. None speaks. They all look at the ground.

"He says he comes in love. But he comes in lust, wanting to see your bodies."

And the women are afraid, for they know that the lust of men is great. But they remember, too, the prophecy passed from mother to daughter, from daughter to granddaughter, to her granddaughter that one day a man would come, would come with a dog, and the dog would not be unclean, and they would walk in the way of peace and love. The women will say nothing now, nothing.

"Take stones from the baskets women. Take stones. You, the tall one, you first, throw a stone at the man. Strike him."

And she is led to the basket by a man. She takes a stone, unwillingly, and walks to the front, standing twenty paces from Morton and Fletch, at the edge of the circle that marks the unclean area. She throws the stone. It goes only a little way, so little, not even close to where Morton looks at her with love and peace in his eyes. She whispers to the man who holds her, "I am weak."

"Another," calls the High Priest. And another woman is taken to the basket of stones, is given a stone, throws it, but it goes only a little way. It does not strike Morton or Fletch. And another woman, another, each saying, "But I am weak." No stone strikes Morton or Fletch.

"They are weak, they say," calls a man at the front. "Then you, you take a stone," the High Priest calls, "and strike the beggar." So the man takes up a stone, he hefts it, and he throws with great force. But the stone goes above Morton's head. It passes high, and Morton is not struck. Fletch looks at Morton, not moving from the place, as close as he can get to Morton. He whines, then yips. They are strong, strong in the love of DOG, the love of the flow of all. The stones will not hit them. Another man, and then another throws a stone, but one goes wide, another sails above their heads, and another lands short, harmlessly, just two paces before Morton. The men are bewildered. They cannot hit the beggar. Never has this happened before. The strongest man with the surest arm then takes a stone, a great rock. He has never missed, always he has been the last, the one to throw the stone that kills. He walks to the front and stops. The High Priest says, "Strike him!" Then the man throws with great force. And the rock goes far to the right, very far. And Morton looks at Fletch, Fletch looks at Morton, and Morton calls out, "There is a way of peace, of love, of kindness, of sharing and giving. Join us my fellows, join us all men and women in the way of peace and love."

Then from the back comes a tall man, thin, irritable, his loose white robes flying as he hurries to the front. Almost running, he hurries. And Fletch howls, the scent of CAT is great upon him. He takes a rock, a large rock from the closest basket. He picks it up, and Morton sees that he has no thumbs, that he grasps the rock with two hands, and he sees the claws, and Fletch howls and growls and barks, and Morton says, "Do you not see, men and women? This is one of the cats of CAT, those that torture and torment you. This is IMPATIENCE, the cat who always pushes to the front, who makes you uneasy at all times. He has no thumbs! Look, his claws! Spurn him! Walk in the way of peace and love, where patience and giving and sharing is all." And they all hear. Some women begin to cry; some men begin to shake. But IMPATIENCE hurries, there at the front, he takes the rock in his hands. Then comes a great shriek, a great shriek from far away, the sound of a mountain lion, far away, beyond the walls but so loud. FERRATSI calls. And IMPATIENCE throws the stone, and it strikes Morton. It hits him hard, in his forehead a great gash.

Then Morton knows the end is near. He looks at Fletch, and Fletch tries to lick him. Then Morton laughs, he thinks of his home, walking with Fletch at the side of Zelda and Rilly, the talk of the way of peace and love, around the fire at night, with all those who know only giving and sharing, and he laughs. Thinking of the way of Ralph, of laughter and joy, he calls out, "Laugh, all, laugh, for there is always joy in love and the way of peace." And Fletch stands up, crippled, on three legs, and yips, he jumps a little, and Morton sings while Fletch yips, "Look on the bright side of life, arf, arf arf, arf arf arf arf arf, look on the bright side of life." Then the men are pushed to the front by IMPATIENCE, and they throw stones, many stones, each hits, Morton and Fletch, each hits, blood then more blood, Morton's face crushed in, Fletch twisted, his spine broken. And with his last breath Morton calls, "Fletch, our mission is done. Father, NAV, we come to thee." And Fletch, in his last breath, barks softly. Then they are dead. But the men continue to throw stones, another and another and another until Morton and Fletch are covered, a great mound of stones. Then all is quiet.

The High Priest calls out, "Leave them there. The mound of stones shows all the end of the way of the infidel." They leave, the men followed by the women three paces back. The square now empty. IMPATIENCE only standing near the circle, sniffing, licking his hand and patting down his hair, again and again, sighing in a mewing sigh. Then he, too, leaves, to join LUST and the High Priest in the temple.

Night comes. A woman appears, without a bearcoat, dressed but her hands and head and feet now free of any cover. She comes, furtively, she comes, and she weeps. She runs, she who had never run, she runs to the mound of stones over Morton and Fletch. Then she takes one stone, one stone, kissing it, weeping, she takes it and she hurries away. Never before had a woman entered the great square uncovered. Then another woman enters from a different path on the other side of the square. Uncovered, too, she hurries to the mound of stones, she takes a stone, she weeps, and she carries it away with her. Then another, and another, each separate, uncovered, scurrying, never more than one in the square. All night the women come, each to take a stone, a stone that would remind them of the way of peace and love.

In the bright light of day, late, the men come out, the High Priest stands on the portico of the temple. He looks at the dusty place, the circle of sand, and he sees nothing. No mound of stones, no head, no body of a dog. The men go to the place where Morton had been put into the ground—the sand is clear, as if never disturbed. They go to the stake where Fletch had been tied—the sand is clear, as if never disturbed. No blood, no hair, no fur, no sign that a beggar and a dog had been stoned there the day before. No sign. But only a sweet smell, a smell stronger than the smell of death lingers in the air.

The Prophecy of Chica

When Tiny returned from his great pilgrimage to the North, the journey to Boris the Second DOGGY LAMA, when Tiny returned to the land of desert and cactus called Aztechoia, he barked to all of the love that DOG has let us learn. He barked of NAV, DOG's only Puppy, sent to earth to teach us how to love, and of Juney, the sweet, the peaceful, the joyful, the First DOGGY LAMA. And he barked of love, of the joy of a loving heart, a love that is greater than death.

They asked of Rosabella, his sister. He told them with sadness and with joy how she had saved him from the terrible cats of CAT, how she had died at the claws of VENGEANCE and FEAR, which FERRATSI, the awful mountain lion, had set upon them. But he had survived, made strong in the love of DOG. He told them how there, in the North, in cold they could not imagine, in snow on the flat tundra now grow two cacti, a prickly pair, always in bloom above the icy casket of Rosabella.

And they were awed. The twitters of the birds, the ravens' caws were true, the calls that told of the love of DOG and of NAV, DOG's only Puppy, sent to teach all sentient beings how to love. They gathered round, all the small almost hairless dogs in the desert night as Tiny told the wisdom and stories of the followers of DOG. And they learned of the great good they must do, to lead humans to learn of love, of trust, of caring. They would go to them. The humans would become less wild, gathering together, learning to trust, hunting as they, the little dogs, yipped and chased the prey. Touching and being touched they would learn to love.

There in the desert they listened, they learned as Tiny told the stories. Much whimpering was joined with many yips of joy as they found their way in the stories and wisdom. Much courage they learned, much courage to bring humans to love, to return violence with love, to live with a loving heart. They learned for many dog-years. Some ventured out, but they returned, still unsure of the way of DOG, until all could tell the stories, all knew the meaning and the power of the wisdom of DOG and of NAV, DOG's only Puppy, sent to earth to teach all sentient creatures to love.

Then they went out, one, and another, and another. They went to the many places in the desert, hot in the sun of the day, cool in the dark of the night, wary, always wary of the cats. And wary, too, of the great deceivers, the cats of CAT, being HATE, GREED, VENGEANCE, LUST, FEAR, GLUTTONY, PRIDE, IMPATIENCE, INDIFFERENCE, SLOTH, SCHADENFREUDE, GUILT, and ALLERGY, who would deceive, leading humans to forsake love for the power that is no power, the power only to hurt, who would follow the way of CAT to destroy all dogs, to destroy the way of love that NAV has taught. Careful, but filled with the joy of love, they went to the places of the humans, they taught the humans of love. They made homes with the humans, guarding, caring, now many generations, many, many dog-years since Tiny had passed into the great flow of all, the flow of love that surrounds us, the great flow of all that is us and is all who have loved, for there is no other, even the cats of CAT can enter the great flow of love if they but want.

Then on the anniversary of the return of Tiny so many, many years ago, at the celebration marked by all who could bark, an old dog, a very old dog, she who is called Chica, once brown now gray, came to the front. Never had she barked around the fire when the stories and wisdom of DOG were told. She had borne so many puppies, so many, generations now, her dugs low, she came slowly to the center. All were surprised, all knew her only as a loving mother, she who had never barked to all. She came forward, did Chica, slowly, for she was old. Then in a beautiful clear bark, she yipped the Great Prophecy.

"There will come a day—you are not ready yet—but there will come a day when some of you will go out, to the South and East, travelling many days. Many will stay here with the humans whom you love and whom you have taught to love with unconditional love. But some will go. You, the tall one, the puppies of the puppies of the puppies of you in the 18th generation, some of them will go. You, the one who is white and black, the puppies of the puppies of the puppies of you in the 19th generation, some of them will go. They will go to the South and to the East to another land, a place where there are great trees, trees so high their tops cannot be seen, where all is green, where there is water that flows in streams, where vines grow fast to cover the path. Some of you will go. And some of you will stay.

And those who go will take the Bark of DOG with you, will go to the great jungle, the green, to find the humans there, the dark ones, short and powerful, you will go to take them the bark of DOG, of love that NAV, DOG's only Puppy has taught us and which we share in our great joy. You will find the humans in the jungle, a jungle with many snakes and with many great cats, but you will have no fear. You will find the cities of the short, dark ones in the jungle, great cities. There you will find temples, square temples climbing higher and higher, with images of CAT upon them. These will be terrible cities where the humans worship CAT in the form of a jaguar, cities that PRIDE makes the humans build, cities where FEAR makes the humans fight other humans, cities where VENGEANCE leads the humans to sacrifice humans they conquer, sacrifice in bloody ceremony. It will be hard, you will suffer, some of you will die, but you will harm no human, harm no dog, for that is the Covenant of DOG. You will go and you will suffer. And your great love will be more powerful than the power of the cats of CAT, more powerful than FEAR and PRIDE and VENGEANCE. You will lead the humans to love. It will take many dog-years, many of you will die, but you will die in the great flow of love, the flow of all."

Chica stopped. She had never before barked to all. She was weary. She coughed. They led her to the bowl of water, they made her sit, they licked her, they spread out for her a small blanket. She rested.

They waited one day and one night. Then another day and another night. They would hear what Chica would say. They were afraid, afraid of the great mission that Chica had told them their puppies would take to the short, dark humans. Would only death be the end of it all?

On the third night, Chica got up, sore, and stretched, and walked slowly to the center near the fire. She stopped, she looked at all, she smelled one then another and another until she had greeted each. Then she began her clear bark.

"You will lead the humans, the short dark ones, the ones who had been deceived by FEAR and PRIDE and VENGEANCE for so long, who had followed the way of CAT, you will lead them to love. Each day, hit or kicked you will return until they see in your eyes the unconditional love we all yearn for. And you will teach them through your unconditional love that they, too, can give unconditional love. You will lead them away from the life of CAT. You will lead them to places deeper in the jungle, away from the temples, so that the temples of the jaguar will fall, the vines will cover the temples of CAT, trees will grow from the rock altars of the human sacrifices, all will fall apart, the center will not hold in the rain and the shaking of the earth. You will lead them to the jungle places, making small villages, homes where each human can know and care for every human and every dog, where they can grow maize and beans and chile and catch the rabbits and sometimes a deer, where there will be enough for all but not so much for PRIDE, where in good years and in bad years the humans will share with each other, will share with you, and will share with all who come to them, FEAR no longer in their hearts."

Then all were glad. This was a mission they would gladly take, though it would not be them, no not for many generations. The puppies of the puppies of the puppies of them in the 18th and 19th generations would begin the mission. This they knew, for they could scent a sweet smell from Chica, a smell of love greater than the smell of death. They knew she barked the future to them, and they knew they would fulfill her prophecy.

Chica stopped. "I have more to bark," she softly yipped, "but I cannot now. I must rest." They went to her, licking her, bringing her the tender parts of the mice and rabbits to eat. She ate little, she needed little, she drank. And she rested. Then on the third night, she began.

"In the jungle you will find a tree, many trees from which a white liquid oozes, white, with a smell that is not good. But the liquid is good, you will find the trees and as the liquid dries you will roll it, round and round, you will roll it. You will push the drying balls of liquid to the fire, baking them at the edge of the fire. Then you will take the ball in your mouth to your human and drop it. You will teach the humans to throw the ball, you will chase it, yipping, then bring it back to them. They will be slow to learn—let them believe they are teaching you, for humans are weak. They will throw, you will chase and return with the ball, and they will laugh. They will have more joy. This will be good."

All the dogs wagged their tails, they yipped, this would be fun. This is grand, for their puppies in the generations to come, to love and be loved, to chase and fetch, a good life they saw.

"Then will be a day when a kitten will come, a small, mewing kitten, so soft, so small, mewing in her stripes and clumsy walk. One of you will have pity, and will take the kitten, will give her of the milk of her own teats, will caress her, remembering that it is possible to lead all sentient creatures to learn to love. The small kitten will be called Puff, and she will be one with you. She will be kind, she will follow you and the humans, and you will learn that all can come to the way of love, that all, even a cat, as she will grow to be, can have a loving heart.

Until the day will come when Puff will hear a call, a mighty shriek from FERRATSI, the mountain lion who answers only to CAT. Then she will go to the jungle. She will be called, and she will learn from FERRATSI, and she will turn to the way of CAT. She will turn to the way of CAT, bringing to the humans plants she finds in the jungle, green plants, that she will place in the fire. The smell will be good to the humans, they will find the plants themselves, they will roll the leaves, they will burn the leaves and take the smoke into their breath, and they will become merry. They will become happy and delighted, but it will be a false delight, an hallucination of love that is not love. And the kitten, now a cat of CAT, will lead them to other plants of green leaves, to more and more, to mushrooms, too, always more powerful, that give strange visions. And the humans will smoke the plants, will eat the mushrooms, and they will become happy and sad, they will forget their way, they will welcome SLOTH and INDIFFERENCE, ugly cats of CAT. They will smoke, they will eat the mushrooms to have the visions they think lead them to DOG but which lead only to CAT, visions that are terrible, visions that are not of love but of false depth, of false insight, of false, of false, of false. And the humans will crave more, they will want always to have these visions they find from the smoking of the leaves and the eating of the mushrooms. They will become weak. And then in the eighth dog-year after the first leaf is smoked, Puff, the kitten, the cat who had known the way of DOG but who had gone to FERRATSI the mountain lion who answers only to CAT, she will become great, she will be taken by FERRATSI to CAT who will give her life without end, life without suffering, CAT will mew, for Puff will now be her cat, the thirteenth cat of CAT, and she will be called ADDICTION."

All was still. All knew that the way of love is powerful, but that the power of CAT is great, too, that CAT can seduce all but the most wary, all but those most strong in the way of love and kindness, of generosity, of sharing. They knew that they, each of them, dog after dog after dog, would teach the humans, and human after human after human who follow in the way of DOG would live to teach the way of love. It is the good way, the only way to live in the flow of all, in the flow of all, sharing, never holding back the pity and the caring whatever the consequences, for it is the way of peace, not the end that matters: there is no way to peace, peace is the way. They knew that no matter the end, they would teach to love, no matter the suffering. They knew that to suffer is to learn more deeply of love. But they were afraid, yes, afraid, for this was a mighty mission and not a happy one when ADDICTION will become powerful among humans.

Then Chica coughed and coughed again. She stumbled. They ran to her, they licked her, she revived, they gave her water. Never before had she barked so long. "My time is short, I must bark the prophecy of DOG that you may know." They wanted to learn. But an old dog, he came to them, he nuzzled Chica. He barked of their young days together, running in the desert, and he lay down beside her. He would not move. He growled when they tried to get Chica to continue. There would be a time, or there would not be a time. Chica must rest, perhaps she will never bark again, but she must rest. And all of them stayed near, though some went and returned, bringing Chica the tender parts of the mice and rabbits to eat.

Chica rested two days guarded always by her mate of long ago, the dog who was the father of so many of her puppies, guarded in the love he gave her. She rested two days. Then she got up and went to the fire. She barked.

"This is the last of the prophecy. There will be no more. Listen carefully.

The dark and small humans will lose their way, but they will never lose your love. Though deep in the ways of ADDICTION, you will love them no less, you will lick them no less, you will be with them always in your unconditional love. They will have this joy if no other.

Then word will come to you of a great horror. Dogs will come to you, fleeing into the jungle from the land of Aztechoia, from all the lands will come dogs. They will tell you of the large humans, of animals you have never seen, of animals so large a human rides upon its back, of sticks that shoot fire, of metal that cuts and cannot be broken, and of dogs, big, hairy dogs, bigger than human children, dogs that attack, that kill humans and kill all dogs who would come between them and the humans. Those who come to the jungle will tell of these humans who are followers of CAT, invaders who have come across the sea in houses that float, humans who are called CATolicos. They will come with FEAR and PRIDE, with GREED and LUST and SCHADENFREUDE at their side to conquer the children of the children of the children—so many generations—of those we live with now, of those we love and who love us, of those for whom we have unconditional love. Their children will suffer, and those who remain here in Aztechoia, the puppies of the puppies of the puppies of you in the generations that come will suffer. These men, hairy, lighter than the humans we know, almost white, they will come with the great animals, with death, with FEAR and PRIDE and GREED and LUST and SCHADENFREUDE, they will come from a land of CAT called CATalunya, to conquer, to kill, to make slaves. Dogs fleeing will come to you, humans, too, fleeing, deep into the jungle. And those of you who can, who have brought your humans back to the way of love, away from ADDICTION and SLOTH and INDIFFERENCE and to the way of a loving heart, you will go deeper into the jungle, to hidden places, away from the power of CAT. There, in quiet places, in hidden places, so deep in the jungle, you will continue the way of DOG, you will tell the stories, you will live in the way of peace and love, you will tell the stories. And you will make the marks we have learned, the marks that tell our stories, you will make them on tablets of the yellow metal, the awful yellow metal that the CATolicos will crave, the yellow metal they believe will give them power. But the yellow metal will not give power, it will be the stories and the wisdom of dog written in the paw prints on the tablets of yellow metal that give the great power of the way of a loving heart. You will live there, hidden, and if discovered never revealing yourself as followers of DOG, for the CATolicos will kill all who are found in the way of DOG. You, in the generations to come, will carry the love in your lives and will be a light unto the multitude when the time of the 4,318th DOGGY LAMA, the first human DOGGY LAMA, comes. And in that time, in that time so many years from now, so many generations we cannot see, you will reveal yourselves again."

Quiet, quiet. All now breathing together in the fullness of the story of what will come. Chica now lying down, her mate of long ago at her side, they look at each other with love, but only for a short while. Then Chica rises to go to her human, to go to José, the one she loves with unconditional love. And her mate rises to go to Juana, his human, the one he loves with unconditional love. All are now filled with the great mission they must remember and tell their puppies so that their puppies will tell their puppies for so many generations. It will come to pass, but how it will come to pass, with only suffering or with love, that is for us to live. We can meet our future with love or hide from it with fear. And FEAR is the most terrible of the cats of CAT.

Recent Writings

At the Animal Shelter

It was a dark and stormy night. Wind and cold. Dark. Still they gathered in the kennel, in the open yard there in what they had heard was called the animal shelter. They all gathered around Rinty, Rinty who was older, who was wise, who knew the stories.

"Tell us, tell us again about Bob," barked a little girl puppy, so soft and silky, tumbling forward to be close to Rinty. And nipping behind her, another puppy, fat and fluffy with brown fur so soft, he yipped, "Tell us about the yard and the bones." And an older dog with a pushed-in face, shaggy silky hair around her eyes, she whined, "Tell us, tell us of the times you went into the hills. Tell us of the times you chased rabbits."

So Rinty spoke to them, in low soft barks, in growls and whimpers, he told them again.

"It was Bob and me, as far back as I can remember, only a faint glimmer of when I was with my mother and some other puppies. A long time ago, so many dog-years. Now I am grey around the muzzle. No one will want me now.

With Bob. Bob would play with me. He held me close to his face and I licked him. He taught me not to make poo in the house. That's an important lesson you'll have to learn, little ones. He took me outside every day. We would walk with him holding one end of the leash."

"What's a leash?" a puppy asked.

"It's a long cord, Bob held one end in his hand and the other he snapped on my collar."

A new puppy asked, "What's a collar?"

"It's a keepsake, something that shows that you and your human are bound together. It shows that he—or she—really cares about you. When you go to the vet—like the one that visits here—they give you shots and then a little tag, and that means your human really loves you. So, a leash. Bob held one end and I took the other in my mouth. It took a really long time to train him to walk with me. Sometimes he went too slow, sometimes he stopped even when there wasn't anything to smell. But he learned. And we walked and walked. There was grass and smells. And somedays we would walk really far to a place where there was no concrete, so far, and he would let me run and run and run. I would smell so many smells, so wonderful, the hills, chasing a rabbit sometimes."

"Is it really possible," said the black and tan puppy, looking so much like Rinty, "to run free like that? To run and run and smell and smell? It sounds wonderful."

And Rinty continued, "Yes, it was good. But better was after the run, with Bob, hugging me, me licking him, wagging my tail so hard my feet moved, then walking back home. And he always stopped at a little pond so I could drink. He never drank with me, though. That was strange.

And best, too, was when Bob met Linda on a walk. She stopped and told him how beautiful I am."

"Ha, ha, ha!" a white rough dog laughed, "You pretty!" And the other dogs all whimpered and some snapped, "Let him tell the story."

"Then Linda came home with us and she lived with us. That was really good. She would press her face into the fur at my neck and make soft sounds, and then scratch me behind the ears, and I would press against her and wiggle. But always my great love was for Bob. Sometimes I dreamt about the moon and wondered why we are here and how the moon power was mine, too. I wanted to be so much. And then I realized I was much. I remember the night . . ." and the little puppies whimpered, afraid.

"I had been looking at the moon, so uneasy. Wanting to do so much. Then I said to myself: Still, there's my devotion. To Bob. Each day. Can that count, too? No greatness there; no moon marking. Yet his life, too, revolves around our love. Me. And him. His strength to me. And me to him. Devotion. Friendship. To ease the hardness in life. No drudgery, yet still hard. Sickness, friendship rejected, love unmet by other love, age, death. Tests enough, for him as me. Always the moon and why the power. For him as me. And death. The final tests. Together. His moods. Rough. Hard. Yet together. Devotion. Friendship. Yet a dog, and not beyond me. Between the grass and the stars. Between. Together."

And all the dogs who had had a human and now were here, they whimpered, they whimpered and whined, remembering. And the little puppies whimpered, wanting and wanting. All wanted to love a human.

Then a brown and red and white little dog, he barked, "I had a human. She was tall, so tall, with brown hair, and a wonderful scent. But she always covered it with some liquid in the morning when she went out, some liquid with an awful smell. I guess she didn't want anyone to know how good she smelled, maybe they would be jealous or want to be with her. She was nice, but she was always gone. It was just a little place, and I was supposed to stay there all day, waiting, waiting. And when she came home she would give me a few pats. Then she would take me down to the street, to the lamp post where I could smell and pee and make poo. Some days we would walk a little, but mostly we would go back to the room and I would sit by her. Sometimes she would pet me. Mostly she looked at something that had a white glow, or held something in her hand to her head and talked. Some days she would even forget to take me outside. But I loved her. I loved her. Then she wanted to leave, a bigger apartment, she said. And she couldn't take me, she said, as she put the leash on me. And she brought me here. I guess I'll wait until she comes back."

And Rinty said, "She won't come back. They never do. I have been here for many days and nights, and I talked to those who were here then and now are gone. Some go to a human, a human comes and wants a dog, and they go home together. But first they take you and cut off your balls, or if you're a girl, they cut you open and take out the stuff you can make puppies with. They do that because they love you, so you won't have puppies that end up here, so you will be closer to your human. It is something you will willingly undergo for the chance to have your own human. Maybe if you are lucky there will be children who will play with you. Yes, hope for that."

And they all whimpered together, almost singing:
>We shall undergo-o-o-o. We shall undergo-o-o-o.
>We shall undergo-o-o-o, some da-a-ay.
>For deep in my nose, I do propose, we shall undergo some day.

"But a lot of us, well, no one would want me. I'm old."

Then a new puppy whimpered, "But why are you here? Did Bob get tired of you? Didn't Linda want you?"

And Rinty said, "They went out one day, on their bicycles. I had to stay in the yard."

"What's a yard?" a puppy asked.

"Shhhh," said an older dog.

"I know," said a big, big dog with powerful jaws. "It's a place with a metal fence around it you can see through, and you're chained up to a post there, and you're supposed to bark at everything that goes by."

And Rinty was sad. "Yes, yes, that's a yard, too. But my yard was different. Lots of grass, big wood fence, smells and flowers and vegetables, and watering it during the summer. And snow in the winter. And a little house for me when they were gone. And I could run and chase and there was a ball for me to play with."

"Heaven." "Yes, heaven." "Oh, that it should be," several whimpered.

"So I was in the yard. But they never came back. Some other people came, people I didn't know. I heard them say that Bob and Linda would never come back, a driver, drunk they said. I don't know what that means. Only I never saw Bob and Linda again. I hope they remember me wherever they are. I loved them so. I still love them so. And now I'm old. No human will want me."

And a young puppy asked, "But what happens if no human wants you? That is horrible. Do we stay here forever, on this concrete floor?"

And another old dog, a shaggy one with hair over her eyes, her eyes watering, her mouth slack, said, "No. I have heard. They take you to that room over there. Then they give you something in a needle. They say that they are putting you to sleep. But no dog ever wakes from that sleep. You are gone forever."

"Horrible." "Horrible." "Horrible." All of the little ones cried and whimpered.

And Rinty said, "You must be prepared for that day. Not everyone is blessed to have a human, a human you can train to love. You have so little time. So many smells, so little time. I will tell you what I know of DOG and the love of DOG through his only Puppy, NAV. I am not wise. I ran with Bob, I pressed up against Linda, I was filled with love. That was my only wisdom. The old ones, the ones that barked to me, told me that this is the great wisdom. But I know only pieces of the stories. I shall tell you."

And they all lay looking at him, some sat, all attentive, sniffing the air, waiting for his bark.

"Be prepared. Whether you find a human, or whether you go to the great sleep, know that DOG loves you and will always love you, whether you are good or bad, He will love you. For the love of DOG is unconditional. And so must the love we give be unconditional. Keep always the Covenant of Dog:

- Be kind.
- Be generous.
- Count not the giving and the taking, but give unconditionally.
- Harm no human.
- Harm no dog.
- Keep from thee hate, greed, vengeance, lust, fear, gluttony, pride, impatience, indifference, sloth, schadenfreude, guilt, and allergy, for these are the way of CAT.
- Put from thee all thought of power save the power of a loving heart.

And then when you die, as we all must die, you will live forever, live in the flow, the great flow of love that gathers us all."

They all were silent, they thought, and the little ones whimpered, and the older dogs barked softly to themselves, repeating the Covenant, those who had known remembering what they had learned when they were young, those who had not known repeating it so they could remember the Bark of DOG.

"And for those of us who will go to the room to be put to sleep, remember to thank DOG for your life. Use the bark of Prometheus, the disciple of NAV, who was the only Puppy of DOG, Prometheus, the bold, so tall, so strong, with massive jaws, full of life, short tan hair, large paws, Prometheus who brought fire to humans, Prometheus who was killed by the cats of CAT—I cannot remember them all, but they are horrible. And when he died, old and torn apart by the cats of CAT, he said what we all should say when we know that we are going to the long sleep:

> Blessed be DOG and His only Puppy NAV that I am grateful
> for the life you have given me. Father, NAV, I come to thee."

And they all repeated it, in small barks, in large barks, gathered together there in the cold and dark and rain and wind on the concrete. And they knew that whether they would be blessed to find a human or whether they would go soon to the long sleep, they were part of the great flow of love that gathers us all, and they would love as best they could, opening their hearts, learning the wisdom of giving.

And some of the puppies, they began to pray. They begged DOG to give them a human, they whimpered. And Rinty said to them, "Pray not. Prayer is only fear and want. Better than prayer is to live in the way of DOG, giving and loving. That is enough for all of us. Remember what we have learned:

There is no hell beneath the earth.
Hell is here, knowing you could have helped but didn't.

There is no heaven above the sky.
Heaven is here, giving with a loving heart."

And they looked at each other, they nuzzled up against each other, smelling each other, licking each other, and then the brown and red and white little dog who had lived in the apartment and would never see his human again, he howled. Not a howl of regret. Not a howl of prayer. But a howl of loneliness. And the others howled with him, and the howls became together a great force, a great binding of them all in love, so that there was no longer loneliness but only the gathering of them in love.

A Report of a Parchment Inscription

[Reprinted in its entirety from the English language newspaper *The Clarion*, City Bell, Argentina, June 18, 1954]

In 1939 and 1940, Reginald G. Farquahar was attached to the British occupation of Palestine as an archaeologist. We have been given access to his notes by the daughter of his sister who resides locally and who wishes to remain anonymous.

The notes explain how in January 1940 Mr. Farquahar came across a single flourishing date palm in an otherwise barren area of sand near the Dead Sea. The locals called it the palm of Kelev Tov, an unusual name which suggested to him the location of an oasis. Superficial digging showed an uneven terrain beneath the surface of sand where he found pottery fragments. After examining those, he began an excavation with the limited resources available to him.

In his notes he details how he uncovered what appeared to be a cemetery in which both dogs and people were buried, some separately, some together. In some of the burials he found pottery with fragments of disintegrating parchment. In one urn, which he dated to between 150 BCE and 50 BCE, he found a piece of parchment about 7.5 inches high by 13 inches wide (18 cm by 32 cm) with an inscription. It would seem from his notes that he found more inscriptions on parchment in pots at that site, but no record or copies of those appear in his papers. He continued the excavation with the help of two Arab assistants, whom he paid himself. Near the cemetery, at the same level, he found remains of a small village. More than 14 feet (4.3 meters) below the surface level and 9 feet (2.8 meters) below the level of the cemetery he found scattered bones of humans and dogs with hack marks and teeth marks on them, suggesting a massacre.

Among his notes was a communication dated August 16, 1940 from the British command in Palestine directing Mr. Farquahar to report immediately for military service. A draft of a letter dated August 22, 1940 from Mr. Farquahar to the military authorities in Jerusalem states that he cannot serve in the military nor aid in any manner the prosecution of war. A peculiar phrase appears in his request for conscientious objector status: "I will harm no human, harm no dog." There is no record of Mr. Farquahar after August 31, 1940 when his Arab assistant Mahmoud bin Ladin delivered to a friend of Mr. Farquahar in Jerusalem a box with the notes of the excavation and the letters described here.

The inscription, which is reproduced below, is in Latin and in a script that appears to be stylized paw prints. It seems that that script is meant to convey the same as the Latin, and it is hoped that this will lead to it being deciphered.

156 The BARK of DOG

The notes, letters, and copy of the inscription, we are assured, will be given shortly to the Archivo General de la Nacion.

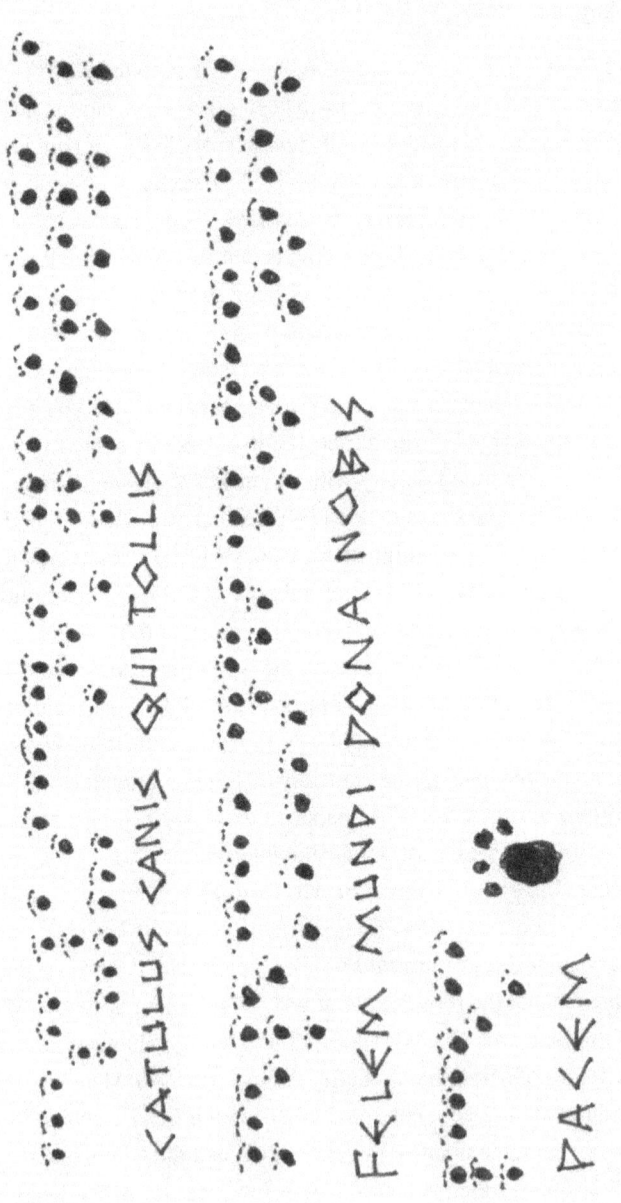

www.ingramcontent.com/pod-product-compliance
Lightning Source LLC
Chambersburg PA
CBHW022106040426

42451CB00007B/138